The Canadian Sioux

The Canadian Sioux are descendants of Santees, Yanktonais, and Tetons from the United States who sought refuge in Canada during the 1860s and 1870s. Living today on eight reserves in Manitoba and Saskatchewan, they have been largely neglected by anthropologists and historians and are the least well known of all the Sioux groups. This study by a long-time student of Sioux and other Indian cultures fills that gap in the literature.

Based on fieldwork done in the 1970s supplemented by written sources, *The Canadian Sioux* presents a descriptive reconstruction of their traditional culture, many aspects of which are still practiced or remembered by Canadian Sioux today although long forgotten by their relatives in the United States. It is rich in detail and presents an abundance of new information on topics such as tribal divisions, documented history and traditional history, warfare, their economy, social life, philosophy and religion, and ceremonialism. Nearly half the book is devoted to Canadian Sioux religion and describes such ceremonies as the vision quest, medicine feast, medicine dance, sun dance, warrior society dances, and the Ghost Dance.

A welcome addition to American Indian ethnography, James H. Howard's study provides a valuable overview of Canadian Sioux culture and a fine introduction to these little-known groups.

The late James H. Howard was a professor of anthropology at Oklahoma State University at the time of his death in 1982. His many publications include *The Warrior Who Killed Custer: The Personal Narrative of Chief Joseph White Bull* (1968, also published by the University of Nebraska Press) and *Shawnee: The Ceremonialism of a Native American Tribe and Its Cultural Background* (1981).

Studies in the Anthropology of North American Indians

Editors
Raymond J. DeMallie
Douglas R. Parks

THE CANADIAN SIOUX
by James H. Howard

University of Nebraska Press
Lincoln and London

Library of Congress Cataloging
in Publication Data
Howard, James Henri, 1925–1982
    The Canadian Sioux.
    (Studies in the anthropology
of North American Indians)
    Bibliography: p.
    Includes index.
    1. Dakota Indians. 2. Indians
of North America—Manitoba.
3. Indians of North
America—Saskatchewan.
I. Title. II. Series
E99.D1H78 1984   971'.00497   83-23506
ISBN 0-8032-2327-7 (alk. paper)

In the interest of timeliness and
economy, this book was printed from
camera-ready copy prepared
by the series editors.

CONTENTS

FOREWORD

Among anthropologists who have studied the cultures and societies of the plains Indians, none can match the breadth and
diversity of field studies of the late James H. Howard. A
native of South Dakota, Howard's interest in the plains Indians
developed during boyhood. He turned to anthropology as the
profession that could provide him with a framework through
which to interpret American Indians. After receiving his
Ph.D. in anthropology from the University of Michigan in 1957,
he taught successively at the University of North Dakota, the
University of South Dakota, and Oklahoma State University.
Howard devoted the entirety of his career to American Indian
studies, including archaeology, ethnology, museum work, ethnohistory, and linguistics. He was a generalist with a consuming
passion to record the traditional cultures of the American
Indian inhabitants of the plains. During the decade preceding
his untimely death in 1982, Howard emphasized studies of dis-
placed tribes from the east which had been removed to present-
day Oklahoma according to the demands of federal Indian policy
in the nineteenth century. His studies embraced an area from
Canada to Oklahoma and varied from the historically-oldest inhabitants of the plains to the latest arrivals. Above all, his
interest was in the interaction of American Indian peoples with
the ecological system of the plains.

    The Canadian Sioux resulted from Howard's ethnographic
survey of the Sioux reserves in Canada. Under the auspices of
the Canadian Ethnology Service of the National Museum of Man
in Ottawa, Howard spent the summer of 1972 visiting each of the
eight Canadian Sioux reserves, attempting to record as full a
picture as possible of all aspects of traditional culture. His

was the first systematic anthropological survey of the Canadian Sioux reserves. Part of the impetus behind the study came from assertions by Sioux people in the United States that their relatives in Canada preserved more knowledge than they of traditional ways. Howard took this as a challenge to record for posterity as much of this traditional knowledge as the Canadian Sioux would be willing to teach him.

Howard's report on his Canadian Sioux fieldwork, combining the data he collected on the Sioux reserves with contextual material from historical and anthropological printed sources, was completed in 1972. It does not attempt to include a comprehensive summary of all previously recorded information about the Canadian Sioux, but rather is a record of traditional knowledge at one moment in time.

For a decade the manuscript remained unpublished. With the inauguration of the University of Nebraska Press series "Studies in the Anthropology of North American Indians," devoted to American Indian ethnography, ethnology, ethnohistory, and linguistics, the editors suggested to Howard that he submit his study of the Canadian Sioux for consideration. While the manuscript was under review, Howard died unexpectedly after a brief illness.

The task of preparing the manuscript for publication was undertaken by the series editors. The original report required some reorganization as well as stylistic editing. The editors regularized linguistic transcriptions and polished English translations. They relied on Eugene Buechel, S.J., A Dictionary of the Teton Dakota Sioux Language, edited by Paul Manhart, S.J. (Pine Ridge, South Dakota: Red Cloud Indian School, 1970), for linguistic reference. Aspirated consonants are followed by a raised, inverted comma (‘); glottalization is represented by a raised comma (’); nasalization is indicated by an eng (ŋ).

The editors added a bibliography and inserted relevant cita-
tions in the text. They also prepared the map. The content
of the work is in every sense as Howard wrote it; the editors'
functions have been organizational and stylistic.

Following University of Nebraska Press convention, the
term "Sioux" is used as the general tribal designation in
place of Howard's "Dakota." The latter term, except when it
appears in quotations from informants, is used in the more
specialized sense to refer to the speakers of Dakota (as
opposed to Lakota). The Wood Mountain Reserve in Canada is inhabited mostly by speakers of Lakota, the Teton dialect; the
other reserves are largely inhabited by Dakota speakers.
Therefore, in referring generally to all of the Lakota and
Dakota speakers in Canada, the expression "Canadian Sioux" is
used.

Many changes have occurred among the Sioux in Canada in
the decade subsequent to Howard's study. Undoubtedly some
traditional knowledge has been lost. At the same time, some
traditional ways have been reintroduced. The Sun Dance, for
example, has been staged at Sioux Valley Reserve, having been
brought there from Standing Rock Reservation in the United
States. The identity of Canadian Sioux people, both as Indians
and as Sioux, has surely intensified during recent years, and
Sioux culture is exhibiting its characteristic strength and
resilience. Very much alive, the culture of the Canadian Sioux
is not static, but is developing into a new phase of existence.
James H. Howard's The Canadian Sioux will stand as a historical
record of this dynamic cultural tradition.

Raymond J. DeMallie
Douglas R. Parks
Series Editors

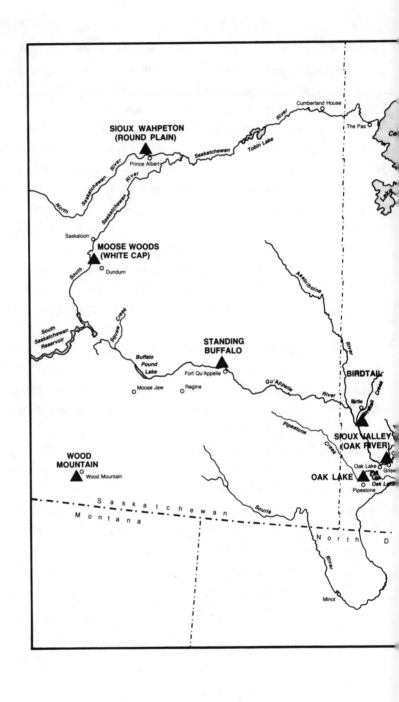

SIOUX WAHPETON
(ROUND PLAIN)

Cumberland House

The Pas

River

Saskatchewan

Tobin Lake

Prince Albert

Saskatchewan River

North

Saskatchewan River

Saskatoon

MOOSE WOODS
(WHITE CAP)

Dundurn

South

Assiniboine

South Saskatchewan Reservoir

Squaw Creek

Buffalo Pound Lake

STANDING BUFFALO

River

Fort Qu'Appelle

BIRDTAIL

Moose Jaw

Regina

Qu'Appelle

River

Birtle

Pipestone

SIOUX VALLEY
(OAK RIVER)

Creek

WOOD MOUNTAIN

Wood Mountain

Oak Lake

Grisw

OAK LAKE

Oak Lake

Pipestone

S a s k a t c h e w a n

Souris

M o n t a n a

N o r t h   D

River

Minot

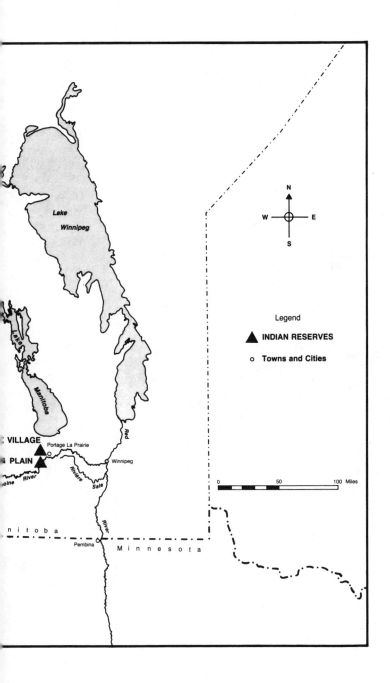

Lake
Winnipeg

Lake
Manitoba

VILLAGE   Portage La Prairie

PLAIN

oine   River   Rivière   Sale   Red

nitoba   River

Pembina   Minnesota

Winnipeg

N
W ⊕ E
S

Legend

▲ INDIAN RESERVES

○ Towns and Cities

0   50   100 Miles

The Canadian Sioux are of interest to the historian for a variety of reasons. They have much the same status as "Treaty Indians," although they have no treaties with the Canadian government. Their presence on Canadian soil is the result of two military campaigns. The first was the campaign of 1862-1863, by which General Henry H. Sibley and his troops put down the so-called "Minnesota Uprising." It resulted in many Santees, or Eastern Sioux, plus a few Yanktonais, fleeing to the "Grandmother's Land" (so named in reference to Queen Victoria), where they felt they would receive fairer treatment than they had experienced in the United States. These Santees and Yanktonais were the ancestors of the Sioux presently located on seven of the eight Sioux reserves in Canada today; namely, Sioux Village (and the Sioux segment of nearby Long Plain Reserve), Sioux Valley (formerly called Oak River Reserve), Birdtail, Oak Lake, Standing Buffalo, Round Plain, and White Cap (also known as Moose Woods). The eighth reserve, Wood Mountain, is populated by descendants of Sitting Bull's band of Hunkpapas. These Western or Teton Sioux are a small remnant of a much larger group that fled to Canada following United States Army campaigns during the 1870s, best remembered in connection with the 1876 Battle of the Little Big Horn. Both of these "wars" are vital parts of the oral historical tradition of the Canadian Sioux, and accounts of episodes involving ancestors in one or the other are still preserved in family traditions.

From an anthropologist's perspective the Canadian Sioux are of considerable interest as well. As Kehoe (1970:149) has noted, the refugee Sioux were enabled, both by the slow expansion of Canadian agriculturalists and the delaying actions of the Métis, to retain their freedom longer than the tribes south of the international border. Thus many aspects of traditional Sioux culture, some long forgotten by their relatives in the States, are still practiced or are a part of the memory culture of the Canadian Sioux. Historically, Canadian federal policy toward Indian citizens differed from that in the United States and fostered a noticeably different attitude toward federal government. Although the present situation of the Canadian Sioux is not drastically different from that of their kinsmen in the United States, a few interesting contrasts are apparent. Certainly the tempo of development has been slower for the Canadian Sioux, and in many cases this seems to have been for the good.

I first became acquainted with the Canadian Sioux in the 1950s through contacts with Indian friends in North Dakota, and I made a few short visits to Manitoba and Saskatchewan reserves in 1953 and 1958. Again in 1968, while doing ethnographic work among the Canadian Plains Ojibwas, I visited four of the Canadian Sioux reserves and interviewed several individuals. The principal fieldwork upon which this monograph is based, however, took place from June 15 through August 15, 1972, during which my wife Elfriede and I were able to visit and interview informants on all Canadian Sioux reserves. This work was made possible by a research contract from the Canadian Ethnology Service, National Museum of Man, National Museums of Canada, whose financial support is gratefully acknowledged. Although two months is too short a time to understand adequately even a single reserve group, I was aided by contacts established earlier; by my ability to speak, to a limited degree, the Dakota language; and by the friendly, outgoing personalities of almost all the individuals we met. Unlike some tribal groups in North America, the Sioux are an easy

people to meet and tend to trust an individual as a friend if
that person demonstrates an interest in their people and their
culture. Of the approximately forty individuals whom I called
upon for interviews, only three refused to visit with me. Of
the remainder, many, on the first or second visit, followed
the old Sioux custom of honoring their visitor with a gift.

Once I had located a potential informant, I asked in Dakota
for the individual's name, to make certain I was addressing
the correct person. Then I identified myself, also in Dakota,
making a few incidental comments on the weather and so forth
before stating my business. This last I generally did in
English. Since the term "anthropology" is not a part of the
vocabulary of most Sioux, I would often say that I was engaged
in collecting "old stories," "Indian history," or information
on "Indian customs." Throughout the interviews I tried to
avoid technical jargon and "big words," and where possible to
use Dakota words and phrases. No set schedule was followed in
the interviews since past experience indicated that the best
information can be secured by merely indicating what sort of
things one is interested in, then letting the informant talk
on whatever aspect of Sioux culture that person finds most interesting and about which he or she is best informed. Once
rapport had been established it was often possible to direct
the interview gently to areas in which I was particularly interested. Heirloom photographs owned by informants often provided a basis for fruitful discussions of old times and a comparison of traditional ways with those of the present. Some
informants preferred to visit with me in private, while others
felt more comfortable when one or two family members or
friends of their same age and sex were present to assist and
correct them. No interview session was continued for longer
than two hours.

Informants who proved to be particularly well informed were, when possible, interviewed two or more times at intervals of a few days to a week. To compensate informants for their expertise and for the time taken from their regular daily activities, small gifts of cash were offered at the close of an interview. Some informants, however, made it very clear that they did not expect or desire such compensation, since I was their guest and on their reserve. Some pressed cash ("gas money"), cuts of venison, fresh vegetables, and other gifts on us to mark the occasion.

In retrospect, I may have attempted too much in trying to cover all eight Sioux reserves in one summer. On the other hand, this enabled me to acquire an overview of Canadian Sioux culture which would not have been possible had I limited myself to a single reserve, or even to the reserves in one province. Still, a greater length of time would have been preferable, and I regret not having been able to visit these communities in the autumn and winter as well as spring and summer. However, I am confident that I was able to acquire a reasonably accurate picture of present day Sioux culture, as well as a fair account of memory culture representing the period of more than a century during which the Sioux have lived in Canada.

1. TRADITIONAL SIOUX CULTURE

Before embarking upon the description of Canadian Sioux culture during the late nineteenth and early twentieth centuries, as well as in the present, it is important to review their ancestral culture as it existed before their flight to Canada. In this I will draw heavily on earlier papers (Howard 1960a, 1966a, 1979, 1980).

Although the Sioux have been known to scholars for more than three hundred years, surprisingly little has been done to collect origin legends and traditional histories from the various divisions of the tribe. Williamson (1851:247) states that the Sioux claimed to have resided near the confluence of the Mississippi and Minnesota Rivers for several generations, and before that to have lived at Mille Lacs. Riggs is quoted as saying that most of the Sioux with whom he conversed could trace their history no further back than to Mille Lacs, but added that all their traditions indicated they came from the northeast and had been moving southwest, implying an origin north of the Great Lakes (Hodge 1907:376). Most present-day scholars would agree in assigning an eastern locale, probably the Great Lakes area, to the Sioux prior to their arrival in Minnesota.

The first published mention of the Sioux was by the French explorer Jean Nicolet in 1640 (Thwaites 1959:231, 233). The first actual meeting between Europeans and the Sioux, however, occurred twenty years later, and took place in what is today northwestern Wisconsin or eastern Minnesota. The principals were the French explorers Pierre Esprit Radisson and Médard Chouart, Sieur des Groseilliers, and a group of Santee Sioux. The explorers, who had spent a miserable winter of near starvation in the vicinity, were visited by eight Santee ambassadors, each accompanied by two women laden with wild rice and corn. The explorers feasted, smoked, and counciled with the Santees for eight days (Radisson 1943:207-209). At this period Sioux territory embraced what is now the southern two-thirds of Minnesota with adjacent parts of Iowa, Wisconsin, and North and South Dakota. Sioux economy was based upon hunting, fishing, and the gathering of lake and forest products, supplemented by some limited horticulture, especially by those bands not having easy access to wild rice.

Partly as a result of pressure from the Ojibwas, who had been armed by the French, and partly because of the attractions it offered in terms of abundant bison and other game, some of the Sioux began a movement westward. By 1750 the westernmost groups had begun to cross the Missouri and filter into the Black Hills region of South Dakota. Until after the War of 1812, most of the Eastern Sioux were allies of the British. Beginning in 1815 they entered into a series of treaties with the United States government.

In 1862 the shabby treatment which the Eastern or Santee bands had received from the government, coupled with the depletion of game by white settlers, led these groups to what has come to be called the Minnesota Uprising. Defeated by government forces, many of the Santees sought refuge in Canada, while others fled west to the Middle and Western Sioux bands. A few Santees were allowed to stay, or later filtered back into Minnesota. Trouble between the Yanktonai band of Middle Sioux and the United States followed, and later the Teton or Western Sioux bands also became involved. These "Sioux wars" culminated in the campaign in which Lt. Col. George A. Custer and his command were annihilated. This last campaign led to the flight of some Tetons, mainly Sitting

Bull's band of Hunkpapas, to Canada, although all but a few
ultimately returned to the United States. In 1890 the last
conflict occurred in connection with the attempt by the U.S.
government to suppress the Ghost Dance religion. Since then
the Sioux have been at peace. Still proud of their military
tradition, the tribe furnished many soldiers for both World
Wars and those in the United States for the Korean and Viet
Nam conflicts as well.

The name Dak'óta is said to mean 'allies'. According to
tradition, the Dakota or Sioux were divided into seven bands
or "council fires," commonly referred to as the Oc'ét'i
Šakówiŋ 'seven fireplaces'. These are the Mdéwak'aŋt'uŋwaŋ,
Waȟpék'ute, Sisít'uŋwaŋ, Waȟpét'uŋwaŋ, Iháŋkt'uŋwaŋ,
Iháŋkt'uŋwaŋna, and T'ít'uŋwaŋ. With the movement of some of
these groups south and west during the late prehistoric and
early historic period, dialectal and cultural differences developed, and three great divisions of the tribe came to be
recognized. The first four of the above-named bands, the
Mdewakantons, Wahpekutes, Sissetons, and Wahpetons, came to be
known as the Santee or Eastern Division. The name Isáŋyat'i
'Dwellers At The Knife' refers to a lake of the Mille Lacs
group where flint for making knives was found. The fifth and
sixth bands, the Yanktons and Yanktonais, came to be known as
the Middle Division, sometimes called Wic'íyena, 'Those Who
Speak Like Men'. The seventh band, the Tetons, became the
Western Division.

The Sioux language is a member of the Siouan linguistic
family. It is divided into three dialects, the "D" or Eastern, "N" or Middle, and "L" or Western. These three letters
refer to a common sound shift found in each. Thus the diminutive suffix -daŋ in the Eastern dialect becomes -na in the Middle dialect, and -la in the Western dialect. Similarly, the

three terms Dak'óta, Nak'óta and Lak'óta were once employed by
the speakers of the three dialects to identify both their own
division and the entire tribe. Thus a Teton will refer to
himself as a Lak'óta and also to the entire tribe as the
Lak'óta. Members of the other two divisions employ the term
Dak'óta in the same way, the form Nak'óta having fallen into
disuse. The Assiniboines and the Stoneys, however, who split
off from the Yanktonais in the not too distant past, still
call themselves Nak'óda when speaking their own language (see
Long 1961).

Culturally, the Santee or Eastern Division of the Sioux
most closely resembled the neighboring Algonquian-speaking
tribes, particularly the Minnesota and Wisconsin Ojibwas, the
Potawatomis, Kickapoos, and Sauks. Their territory, roughly
speaking, embraced the southern two-thirds of present Minnesota, with adjacent portions of Wisconsin, northern Iowa, and
eastern North and South Dakota. Aboriginally, it was a land
of lakes and forests, interspersed with large areas of park-
land and prairie.

The economy of the Santees was nicely adjusted to their en-
vironment, and rested upon a base of hunting, fishing, gathering, and horticulture. The first two of these activities were
carried on by men, the last two largely by women. The Santees
hunted bison locally, and mounted organized hunting expedi-
tions to the west to secure this animal, but buffalo hunting
was certainly not so important to them as it was to the Middle
and Western divisions. Deer, elk, and moose were the most
common quarry. The lakes and streams of the area provided a
variety of fish. Spear fishing took place at river rapids and
on lakes. At night, birchbark and pitch torches aided the
spearmen. Large nets were also employed in lake fishing. Important wild vegetable foods were wild rice, maple sugar, and

t'ípsiŋna, a starchy root. In some communities women tended
large gardens of corn, beans, squashes, and pumpkins (Skinner
1919:167). The amount of gardening done by the Santees, however, seems to have been inversely proportional to the avail-
ability of wild rice near a particular village. If wild rice
were readily available, it provided the main source of vegetable food and gardening was neglected. The late George Will,
in his studies of American Indian corn, found a distant variety in the possession of the Canadian Santees (personal communication, 1951), which would seem to indicate that corn horticulture was a complex of respectable antiquity among the
Santees.

The common summer dwelling of the Santees was a large
gable-roofed house of poles and bark called the t'ípi t'áŋka
'big lodge' (Mayer 1932:104-108). In winter, small hemispher-
ical cattail mat or bark wigwams were used, as well as skin
covered tipis much like those of the Middle and Western divisions. The tipi tanka had a sleeping and lounging platform
about five feet wide and two and a half feet above the ground
extending around the inside of the house (Mayer 1932:165).
Braided cornhusk floor mats and woven cattail mats were used
to cover the floors and the lounging platform and to line the
walls (Skinner 1919:165). Over the door, located at one end
of the tipi tanka, was a roof or shed extending some eight or
ten feet from the building and supported by posts. This
served as an outside lounging platform and was also used for
drying corn and other vegetables. On hot summer nights it
served as a sleeping platform. A medicine pole usually stood
near each lodge (Mayer 1932:108-109). Because they lived
south of the canoe birch area, the Santees generally employed
dugout canoes. When not in use these were sometimes stored on
top of the shed of the tipi tanka.

The village was the principal Santee social unit. Some
villages maintained the same name and location over long periods of time, when family lines survived for generations
(Landes 1968:31). The village was composed originally of
close kin, perpetuated in offspring. It would appear that
villages tended to be exogamous and that patrilocality was the
preferred post-marital residence pattern. Each village was
governed by a chief, whose position was permanent. Village
chieftainship tended to be hereditary, passing from a father
to his eldest son. As leader of the village, a Santee chief
possessed some prestige but little coercive power, governing
largely by friendly persuasion. Each chief appointed as his
executive officer a head akíc'ita 'soldier', perhaps better
expressed in English as "policeman" (Skinner 1919:173). This
man's duty was to keep order in the village and to enforce the
orders of the village chief. Both the chief and the head soldier depended ultimately on the village council for their authority. This council was apparently made up of all the adult
males in the village, although the details of its composition
are unknown.

In time of war or other emergency the village chief might
yield control to a war chief, an experienced warrior who might
or might not be the same man as the peacetime head soldier.
Sources are unclear as to how the war chiefs were selected,
but one gathers that many of them were strong personalities
who simply usurped their power. During emergencies the council appointed additional akicita, who, with the war chief,
made up the t'iyót'ipi or soldier lodge. This group met
daily in a special lodge erected for their use in the center
of the village. Here they counciled, sent and received mes-
sages, and feasted. Among the Santees, akicita were selected
from various warrior societies on the basis of personal merit.

An entire warrior society was never selected for akicita duty, as was the case with the Tetons.

Although each Santee village was largely autonomous--politically and economically--the village group might join with other Santee villages, or even with Yankton and Yanktonai groups, on the tribal bison hunt. To maintain order on the hunt the village council, or a council of the combined village groups, would select one or more hunt chiefs. For the duration of the hunt, these men were in complete charge, possessing dictatorial powers. Like the war chief in time of war, the hunt chief temporarily outranked even the village chief. The hunt chiefs were assisted by a number of akicita and the tiyotipi was set up just as when the village went to war. The akicita patrolled constantly, and if any individual hunters went ahead of the main group to hunt and thus scared the game away, the soldiers whipped them and also cut to pieces the offenders' lodge covers and other belongings. The authority of the hunt chiefs and akicita lasted only for the duration of the hunt, after which they resumed their ordinary status. Organized deer hunts, similar to bison hunts but on a much smaller scale, were described by Landes' Santee informants (1968:53-55). Often both war chief and hunt chief were powerful shamans who claimed supernatural assistance in carrying out their missions.

In their dress, the Santees more closely resembled the Ojibwas, Potawatomis, Kickapoos, and other Algonquian tribes than the Sioux groups to the west. Men generally banged their hair in front and cut it short in back, braiding the remainder into four braids, two of which fell on either side of the forehead and two behind the ears. The Wahpetons are said to have roached their hair in the past (Skinner 1919:164). Old photographs show a variety of headdresses used by Santee men,

including the porcupine guard hair and deer tail roach headdress and the finger-woven sash turban, both of which were
often worn together. Sometimes a wide cloth "crown" decorated
in floral beadwork was worn in place of the sash turban.
Another distinctive style of headdress, also used by the Ojibwas, Winnebagos, and Prairie Potawatomis, consisted of an otter skin fillet in which four bone cylinders, holding eagle
feathers, were arranged at equidistant points. An ornate capouche or hood was also worn (Winchell 1911:figure 14, opposite 504). Sometimes this hood was sewn directly to the hunting coat, in which case it is termed a capote. In winter the
hood warmed the ears and in summer it kept off mosquitoes
(Mayer 1932:126-127, 130). Similar hoods were worn by the
Ojibwas, Crees, and Winnebagos. According to Skinner (1919:
164) the Plains warbonnet was also used to some extent by the
Santees, but it does not appear frequently in the older photographs.

Originally, Santee men's shirts were made of buckskin,
rather close fitting, and unfringed. Later, cloth shirts of
a similar type, decorated with beadwork and/or ribbonwork,
came into use. The breechcloth was of the type passing between the legs and hanging over the belt a foot or so in front
and in back. Leggings were of the front seam type, with large
flaps projecting out above the knees, but tailored to fit
tightly below, and equipped with flaps extending over the
moccasin tops in front. Finger-woven sashes and kneebands
were also in general use. Kneebands made from the entire skin
of a small otter were also worn. Carver illustrates a
"Naudowessie" (Sioux) man wearing a peculiar triangular-shaped
knife sheath on his chest (Parker 1976:96), which seems to
have been characteristic of the Santees. It appears almost a
century later in portraits of the famous chief Little Crow.

Another favorite item of adornment was the grizzly bear claw
necklace.

The oldest style of Santee moccasin was soft-soled, puckered to a single seam at the top, and equipped with very large
ankle flaps (Skinner 1919:169). Later the Ojibwa style moccasin with smaller ankle flaps and a beaded tongue piece came
into general use. A third type, still used by the Canadian
Santees, seems to be a combination of the two styles above.
It has a single seam extending from the toe about half way up
the top of the foot, then a small tongue piece. All three
types are excellently suited for stalking game on a Woodland
underfooting of pine needles and moss, and would be poor protection against the prickly pear and bunch grass stubble of
the High Plains.

Santee women wore the two-piece Central Algonquian style
dress consisting of a wrap-around skirt ornamented with ribbonwork applique at the hem and up the front, and a loose
blouse (Skinner 1919:164). These blouses were often ornamented with a profusion of metal brooches or beadwork. Santee
women generally wore their hair in a single braid down the
back and ornamented this with a bead wrapping from which hung
many ribbons or oblique beaded bands. Several strands of
beads were usually worn about the neck, jet being a favorite
color.

Curvilinear floral designs became popular with the Santees
during the nineteenth century, almost completely replacing the
older geometric motifs. At the present time such "flower
beadwork" is still seen on both men's and women's dancing costumes, but Plains style geometric designs are equally popular,
and sometimes both styles appear on the same piece. There are
at least three general types of floral beadwork made by the
Santees. One type is almost identical with the realistic

floral work of the Minnesota Ojibwas, and is generally done on
black velveteen or with a filled-in white bead background.
The Santees, however, are quite fond of inserting an occasional butterfly, bluebird, or deer motif amongst the realistic
flowers. A second type of floral beadwork (and quillwork)
utilizes finer design elements and balances these in bilateral
symmetry. The third type utilizes large stylized floral designs of the Winnebago and Potawatomi type, often in crystal
beads.

The Sissetons and Wahpetons, sometimes termed the "Upper
Council" Santees, were more Plains-like in their dress than
the "Lower Council" Mdewakantons and Wahpekutes. Sisseton men
frequently wore their hair in two braids, one at either side
of the head, just behind the ears, a common Plains style.
These braids were wrapped in otter skin. Likewise, Sisseton
shirts and leggings were often Plains-like, with long fringes,
and their moccasins were of the hard-soled Plains type (Skinner 1919:165).

Archaeological sites in Minnesota attributed to the Santees
yield pottery of Woodland type, which corresponds to the account of pottery making recorded by Skinner (1919:165). According to his informants, all of the Santee bands traditionally made pottery of pounded clay tempered with crushed rock.
Decoration was applied by stamping the unfired vessel with a
carved paddle. Before firing, the vessel was smeared with
glue. Skinner's informants also recalled that their ancestors
had formerly used flint knives, scrapers, and arrow-points,
as well as similar objects of bone. He collected a double-
pitted hammerstone that was still in use. These informants
also mentioned the use of grooved mauls and grooved stone axes
to break up firewood--Woodland archaeological culture traits
that apparently survived until a very late date with the

Santees. Smaller mauls were used to crush berries, and chip-
ped flint axes were used to chop wood. Horizontal wooden mor-
tars of Central Algonquian type were used to pound corn. Distinctively Santee pestles were merely crude, heavy sticks
(Skinner 1919:166).

Wooden bowls with tastefully carved animal head decorations
were reserved for use in the Medicine Dance and Medicine
Feast. A few of these are still preserved among the Canadian
Santees. Both wood and bison horn spoons were manufactured
(Skinner 1919:165). Santee men followed the old circumpolar
custom of carrying wooden noggins and spoons fastened to their
belts by means of toggles.

Like their Algonquian-speaking neighbors, the Santees wove
bags of cedar and basswood fibers. Square woven tobacco
pouches, which Skinner notes as a Central Algonquian style,
were worn about the neck. Willow withe baskets were made by
all four Santee bands, as were birchbark vessels. The Mdewakantons and Wahpekutes used barrel-shaped hide parfleches, the
Sissetons and Wahpetons a box type and a flat rectangular type
more reminiscent of the Plains (Skinner 1919:166). Tumplines
of moosehide were used in back packing and by women in carrying the cradle board. Santee cradle boards were of the solid
piece style typical of the Eastern Woodlands (Mayer 1932:126,
Skinner 1919:166).

The principal Santee weapon for both hunting and war was
the bow and arrow. Santee bows were of the self type, about
three and a half feet long, generally made of ash wood with a
twisted sinew bow string. For close fighting the ball-head
and rifle-stock types of warclub were employed (Skinner 1919:
166). Both the ball-head type warclub and a characteristic
triangular dagger (contained in the chest sheath mentioned

above) are pictured by Carver in the oldest known sketch of a Sioux Indian (Parker 1976:96-97).

Among the musical instruments of the Santees were the single and double headed tambour or hand drum and the tall wooden water drum. The latter, a typical Woodland Indian instrument, was apparently used for all major ceremonies, including the Medicine Dance and the Sun Dance (Eastman 1849: xxii). The Grass Dance drum, which in size and shape approximates a bass drum, apparently reached the Santees in 1847 or 1848 when they adopted the Grass Dance from the Winnebagos. Musical rasps of bone, with tin plate resonators, are described by Eastman (1849:xx). The tin plate resonators had very likely replaced aboriginal ones of gourd. Deer hoof and gourd rattles were also used, the latter especially by shamans and in the Medicine Dance. Mnemonic song records were either incised on flat boards or birchbark sheets, and were used mainly to record the sequence of Medicine Dance songs.

Deer hides were dressed over an inclined log in Algonquian style, but bison hides were staked on the ground for tanning, a practice more typical of the Plains. Both elk antler and wooden scrapers were used to tan buffalo robes (Skinner 1919: 167-168).

Popular Santee field games were snow snake, lacrosse, and shinny. Most gambling by men was done via the moccasin game. Women preferred "plum shooting," in which plum seed dice were shaken in a wooden bowl. Telling folktales was a common winter pastime. The folklore of the Santees is very similar to that of the Ojibwas and Potawatomis (see Wallis 1923). One important exception is that Uŋktómi 'Spider', the culture hero Trickster, does not seem to be connected in any way with the Medicine Dance. Other prominent folkloristic characters include the Double Woman and Little Tree Dweller. Tales of Windigo-type cannibals are also present.

The chief ceremonies of the Santees were the Medicine Dance, which closely resembles and is probably derived from the Midewiwin of the Ojibwas and Sauks; Sun Dance; Thunder Dance; Medicine and Adoption Feasts; and the Little Tree Dweller ritual. Various warrior-dancing societies of the Prairie and High Plains type were present. A secularized form of one of these, the Grass Dance, survives at the present time (see Howard 1951). A distinctively Santee dancing society was called the "Raw Fish Eaters." Members dressed and danced in imitation of the cormorant (Lowie 1913:123-124).

Carver mentions a ceremony, already obsolescent in his time, involving sexual intercourse of a ritual nature. This rite was known as the Wild Rice Feast, and may have been performed to ensure the fertility of this important staple. A young unmarried woman of high rank invited the most respected warriors of the village to her lodge. There they feasted on wild rice mixed with bear grease, danced, and each lay privately with the woman on a bed prepared at one side of the tent (Parker 1976:108). The woman was thereafter held in great respect by the tribe and subsequently married a prominent man.

The Santees were the only Sioux division among which the institution of brideservice was recorded. This probably reflects an economy in which it was difficult to accumulate sufficient capital goods to purchase a wife. A youth, when he had selected a girl as his bride-to-be and had reached an agreement with her parents, went to live for a year in their house, hunting and performing menial tasks for the family. If he demonstrated during this time that he was able to support a wife, he was formally married to the girl at a public feast, which concluded with the groom carrying off the bride on his back (Parker 1976:106).

The Santees were considered by other Sioux to be great
magicians and shamans, with power to change themselves into
birds and fly through the air, to walk on hot coals, and to
compound lethal medicines to kill enemies or seduce women.
Members of the Medicine Dance and Heyoka cult, particularly,
were thought to be great wonder-workers. The characteristic
plant of the Santee shaman was the fern, rather than the sage
of the Middle and Western divisions. The floor of the lodge
in which a shaman conducted a curing ritual was covered with
ferns. Sweetgrass was also a very important plant to the
Santees. Its smoke was thought to be pleasing to the Thunderbirds, hence it was often burned when a storm approached to
mitigate the destructive effects of the tempest.

Two forms of burial were practiced by the Santees. In the
first, the body was buried in the ground and a small house was
built over the grave. This was also practiced by the Ojibwas,
Potawatomis, and Winnebagos. Sometimes mounds were erected
over such graves. In the second type of burial, the corpse
was placed on a scaffold or platform in a tree, a trait more
characteristic of the Plains area.

2. TRIBAL DIVISIONS

Traditional Band Names

Most Canadian Sioux are descendants of refugees from the Minnesota Uprising and belong to the four Santee bands. In addition there are a few Yanktonais on the Birdtail and Oak Lake
reserves and the majority of the Sioux at Wood Mountain are
descended from the Hunkpapa sub-band of the Tetons. In their
homeland, each of the four Santee bands was divided into sub-
bands, as were the Yanktons, Yanktonais, and Tetons. Most
adult Canadian Santees today are still able to give their band
affiliation (whether Mdewakanton, Wahpekute, Sisseton, or Wahpeton), but sub-band identities have become blurred or completely forgotten. In fact, although most informants were
familiar with some sub-band names and traditional origins and
might identify a particular family with one or another group,
they tended to equate sub-bands with bands. The following
outline, therefore, necessarily relies upon the account given
by Riggs (1893:156-161).

Mdéwak'aŋt'uŋ or Bdéwak'aŋt'uŋ 'Spirit Lake Dwellers'

This Eastern Sioux band is said to have taken its name from
its former place of residence at Mille Lacs in Minnesota,
which the Sioux called Mdéwak'aŋ or Bdéwak'aŋ 'Sacred Lake'.
Riggs lists seven sub-bands (which he calls "gentes"): (1)
K'iyúksa 'Breakers Of Custom Or Law'; (2) Ḣemníc'aŋ 'Hill-
Water-Wood', referring to Barn Bluff at Red Wing, Minnesota;
(3) Kap'ója 'Light Ones', those who travel unemcumbered with
baggage; (4) Magáyutesni 'They Who Do Not Eat Geese'; (5)
Ḣeyátat'uŋwe 'Back Villagers'; (6) Oyáte Šíca 'Bad People';
and (7) T'íŋtat'uŋwe 'Prairie Villagers'.

According to my Canadian Sioux informants, there are a few
people of Mdewakanton descent at Sioux Valley and Round Plain,

and the majority of Sioux on the Birdtail Reserve are of this
band. Most of the Mdewakantons, however, ended up on various
reservations in the United States. Their descendants are now
found on the Lower Sioux Reservation, near Morton, Minnesota;
Upper Sioux Commission, near Granite Falls, Minnesota; Prairie
Island Settlement, near Red Wing, Minnesota; Prior Lake Reservation, near Mankato, Minnesota; Flandreau Reservation in
South Dakota; and the Santee Reservation in Nebraska. Some
individuals at Fort Totten, North Dakota, on the Devil's Lake
Reservation, are also Mdewakantons (Louis Garcia, personal
communication).

Of the various sub-bands listed above, only two were remembered by my informant Robert Good Voice (Round Plain) who
is Mdewakanton on his father's side and Wahpeton on his
mother's. These were Hill-Water-Wood and They Who Do Not Eat
Geese. He explained that the latter name originated because
the members of this sub-band commonly sold the geese they
killed to settlers rather than eating them themselves. The
band name Mdewakanton, he said, derived from the fact that
these people once lived at a lake where they periodically
heard a mysterious voice. He had no idea where the lake might
be or what it was called in English. The generic term for the
Eastern Sioux, Isanti (Santee), Mr. Good Voice explained, derived from the fact that these people once lived near a cliff
where they quarried flint for knives.

Wahpék'ute 'Leaf Shooters'

This Eastern Sioux band has been closely associated with
the Mdewakantons since 1851 (Riggs 1893:157). Accordingly,
Wahpekute are often found on the same reserves where there are
Mdewakantons, including Sioux Valley and Round Plain. According to John Goodwill there are also a few at Standing Buffalo

Reserve. They are in the majority at Oak Lake, where some are descendants of Chief Íŋkpaduta 'Scarlet Point', who attained notoriety for the 1857 Spirit Lake Massacre in Iowa. One such descendant, Mrs. Arthur Young, was my informant. No stigma whatever attaches to the Inkpaduta connection among the Canadian Sioux. Other Wahpekute descendants are found on the Santee Reservation in Nebraska and at Fort Peck, Montana. The combined Mdewakanton and Wahpekute bands are sometimes collectively termed the "Lower Sioux Council."

Sisít'uŋwaŋ (Sisseton) 'Ridges Of Fish Offal Dwellers'

This Eastern Sioux band is said to have taken its name from the fact that they caught many fish in the rivers and lakes when they lived at Traverse des Sioux, Blue Earth, and Cottonwood, in Minnesota. They cut up and dried the fish, throwing the scales and entrails in heaps, which appeared partly white and shining and partly black and dirty. This appearance was termed siŋsíŋ in Dakota, from which their name derived (Riggs 1893:158). I recorded the same story as part of Sioux oral tradition from Ella Deloria, the Yankton Sioux linguistic anthropologist, and from Sam Buffalo at Round Plain. Mr. Buffalo added that this was a name of derision originally, and that it was the type of name often invented and bestowed on a group by a wíŋkte (homosexual) to make people laugh.

Sub-bands of the Sissetons listed by Riggs are: (1) T'izá-ptaŋna 'Five Lodges'; (2) Ok'óp'eya 'In Danger'; (3) C'aŋsda-cík'ana 'Little Place Bare Of Wood'; (4) Amdówapuskiya 'Driers On The Shoulder'; (5) Basdécesni 'Those Who Do Not Split (the backbone of the buffalo)'; (6) Kap'ója 'Light Ones'; and (7) Ohdíhe (not translated). Edward Ashley (Riggs 1893:159) gives a different listing, including the C'aŋk'úte 'Shooters At Trees', another name given in derision. Of the above, one or

another of my informants remembered four sub-bands, Five
Lodges, Driers On The Shoulder (in the form Abdowapuskiya),
Light Ones, and Shooters At Trees.

From the Sioux at Fort Totten, where the Five Lodges sub-
band is well represented, Louis Garcia (personal communication) secured a story explaining the traditional origin of
this group. Long ago a Sioux man had five grown sons, one of
whom abducted a woman. Fearing pursuit, this man, together
with his four brothers, separated from the main camp. Relatives and friends of the kidnapped woman found the five brothers and attacked their camp, and several people were killed.
Peace was finally restored by the headmen but the five brothers and their following continued to dwell apart. This sub-
band is prominent at Fort Totten, where Holy Standing Buffalo
Cow was headman of the group. At Fort Totten the Red Fox,
Young, Merrick, Little Wind, Woods, and Longie families are
of this sub-band. Some also live at Sisseton, South Dakota.
In Canada the Bob Royal family at White Cap Reserve belongs to
this group.

The Driers On The Shoulder sub-band lived at Lake Traverse
and were great buffalo hunters. They often moved camp when
their meat was not yet dried and so spread it out on the
horses' backs and on the thills (travois), and from this custom received their name (Riggs 1893:159). At Fort Totten
Louis Garcia was told a similar story, but in this version the
sub-band was butchering buffalo when the enemy came near.
They therefore tied sticks on their horses' necks, parallel to
their backs, and put the meat there to dry during their retreat. I recorded a similar story at Standing Buffalo Reserve, where this sub-band is well represented. Riggs notes
that Standing Buffalo and his people were of this sub-band
(1893:159). He has many descendants on the Standing Buffalo

Reserve today, including my informant Martha Tawiyaka. At
Fort Totten Mat'ó Hín 'Bear's Hair' was chief of this sub-
band. The present One Bear, Lawrence, and Adams families are
of this affiliation. I was told that some members of this
sub-band are to be found at Sioux Valley, Round Plain, and
White Cap reserves, and also at Fort Peck, Montana.

The Light Ones sub-band of the Sissetons, like the Mdewakanton group of the same name, acquired their title because
they traveled with very little baggage. The Martin family at
Standing Buffalo Reserve is of this sub-band.

The Shooters At Trees sub-band is represented at Standing
Buffalo, White Cap, and Round Plain. No information was secured as to the circumstances that caused this group to be so
named.

Wahpét'uŋwaŋ (Wahpeton) 'Leaf Dwellers'

Riggs (1893:157) notes that this band probably obtained its
name from the fact that they formerly lived only in the woods,
and that their old home was at Little Rapids, Minnesota. Ed-
ward Ashley, a missionary to this band, obtained the following
list of sub-bands in 1884 (Riggs 1893:158, footnote 1): (1)
Iŋyaŋc'eyaka At'úŋwaŋ 'Village At The Rapids'; (2) Tabkápsiŋ
T'uŋwáŋna 'Those Who Dwell At The Shinny Ground'; (3) Wiyáka
Ot'ína 'Dwellers On The Sand'; (4) Ot'éhi At'úŋwaŋ 'Village
On The Thicket'; (5) Wíta Ot'ína 'Dwellers In The Island'; (6)
Wakpá At'úŋwaŋ 'Village On The River'; and (7) C'aŋkága
Ot'ína 'Dwellers In Log (huts?)'.

None of these sub-bands were remembered by my Canadian
Sioux informants, but Louis Garcia reports that the Dwellers
In The Island sub-band is remembered at Fort Totten. Just as
the Mdewakantons and Wahpekutes are known collectively as the
"Lower Council" of the Santees, so the Sissetons and Wahpetons
are termed the "Upper Council." Today it is extremely diffi-

cult to separate these pairs of bands because of long co-residence and intermarriage.

In our separate investigations, Louis Garcia and I have found reference to three more sub-bands not listed by Riggs or Ashley for either the Sissetons or Wahpetons. They are Hiŋta Haŋkpá 'Basswood Legging String'; Išpá T'ahíŋspa 'Needle Elbow'; and C'usdípa 'Dew Lickers'.

According to a story recorded by Garcia, the Basswood Legging String sub-band originated from an incident in which a Sioux girl was eloping with a youth from another village. During their flight the couple stopped to have intercourse. As she was dressing, the girl found that her legging string or garter was missing. They did not linger to search for it, knowing that the girl's family was in pursuit. Instead, the girl stripped off a piece of basswood bark, a common material for cordage among the Sioux, and used it as a garter. When the pair arrived at the young man's village his relatives welcomed them. Following Sioux custom, his female relatives proceeded to dress the girl in a fine new costume. While doing this the women noticed the basswood fiber legging string. It was considered an amusing happenstance and hence the descendants of the couple were given this distinctive name referring to the incident. At Fort Totten, Left Bear was chief of this sub-band. The Blue Shield, Iron Hawk, Gray Wind, Courts, and Thompson (Michael) families belong to this sub-band. The group is represented in Canada at Round Plain and Sioux Valley. At the latter reserve my informant James Kiyewakan claimed this affiliation.

The Needle Elbow sub-band also takes its name from an amusing incident. Two or three sisters were married to the same man. Usually sisters involved in a sororal polygynous marriage got along well together, but these sisters did not.

Jealous, they constantly poked each other with their elbows as they sat together in the tipi. On one occasion one of them cried out that the other had an elbow as sharp as a needle. The remark was overheard and provided a derisive name for the lineage. At Fort Totten, Arm Bag was chief of this sub-band. The Jackson, Abraham, Guy, Mibebe, Raven, Gourd, Cavanaugh, Hunts, Iron Heart and Peoples families are members of this lineage on Devil's Lake Reservation. On the Standing Buffalo Reserve this sub-band is also well represented and includes the Tawiyaka family. It is also present at Round Plain.

The name Dew Lickers was bestowed because of an incident in which the members of this sub-band, unable to find drinking water while on the march, licked the morning dew from the grass to quench their thirst. It is well represented at Standing Buffalo Reserve, where the Whiteman family is of this affiliation. It was formerly prominent at Round Plain, according to Sam Buffalo, but all of its members died in the 1918 influenza epidemic. Because of this it is common for Round Plain Sioux to refer to the pre World War I era as "the days of the Dew Lickers."

In addition to the above, there are also Sissetons of indeterminate sub-band at the Upper Sioux Indian Commission near Granite Falls, Minnesota, and Wahpetons at Flandreau Reservation in South Dakota; on the Birdtail, Sioux Valley, Sioux Village, and Oak Lake reserves in Manitoba; and at Round Plain Reserve in Saskatchewan. The latter is sometimes called the Wahpeton Reserve. Laviolette (1944:114) indicates that the Wahpetons at Sioux Village, near Portage La Prairie, are members of the Dwellers On The Sand sub-band.

Iháŋkt'uŋwaŋna (Yanktonais) 'Little Dwellers At The End'

Of the two Middle Division bands, only the Yanktonais are represented among the Canadian Sioux, a few of whom live at

Oak Lake and Birdtail reserves in Manitoba. George Bear, from
the latter reserve, identified himself as Yanktonai. No sub-
bands were remembered by my informants at either of these two
reserves. In Canada, as in Montana and North Dakota, members
of the Yanktonai band are inclined to call themselves "Yanktons" when speaking English, ignoring the diminutive suffix
-na at the end of their Dakota name. There may be a few Yanktonais at Sioux Valley, since a sub-band named T'ahúha Yúta
'Eaters Of Hide Scrapings' was remembered by Eli Taylor of
that reserve. This name appears historically as a Lower Yanktonai sub-band (Riggs 1893:161 footnote 1).

T'ít'uŋwaŋ (Tetons) 'Dwellers On The Prairie'
All but seven of the Sioux people at Wood Mountain Reserve
are Tetons, members of the Hunkpapa sub-band. Through intermarriage, individuals of part Teton descent are also found on
the Standing Buffalo Reserve.

The Canadian Reserves

Map 1 shows the locations of the eight Canadian Sioux reserves. The population figures given below are as of December
31, 1971.

Manitoba

Sioux Village (near Portage La Prairie)	235
Sioux Valley (near Griswold)	956
Birdtail Sioux (near Birtle)	203
Oak Lake (near Pipestone)	281

Saskatchewan

Standing Buffalo (near Fort Qu'Appelle)	512
White Cap or Moose Woods (near Dundurn)	156
Round Plain or Sioux Wahpeton (near Prince Albert)	86
Wood Mountain (near Wood Mountain)	70
Total Population	2,499

About one-third of the total population resides off the re-
serves, although this varies seasonally and from year to year.
The Sioux names of the various reserve localities are:
Sioux Village, T'ipó Iháŋke 'Farthest Camp', so named from the
fact that at one time this was the farthest extension of the
Sioux to the north and west; Sioux Valley, Wipázuk'a Wakpá
'Juneberry Creek'; Birdtail Sioux, C'aŋkáǧa Ot'í 'Dwellers In
Log Cabins', so named because this group was the first to
build and live in this type of dwelling; Oak Lake, C'aŋdúpa
Wakpá 'Pipe Creek', so called because when the Sioux first
came to this locality they found a pipestone pipe at an abandoned Plains Cree or Plains Ojibwa camp; another name for this
locality is Wic'áp'aha Iyéyapi 'Where They Found The Scalp',
so called because when the Sioux first came here they found a
human scalp stretched on a hoop, the whole affixed to an upright stick that was stuck in the ground; Standing Buffalo,
T'at'áŋka Nájiŋ 'Standing Buffalo Bull', named after the chief
of the band that settled there; White Cap or Moose Woods,
Wap'áhaska 'White Warbonnet', also named after the chief of
the band that settled there; Round Plain or Sioux Wahpeton,
T'íŋtamibena 'Round Plain', named for the locale of the reserve, an open place in the woods; Wood Mountain, C'áŋowaŋcaya
Pahá 'Forest Mountain'.

The original chiefs on the various reserves were: Sioux
Village, Oínajiŋ 'Cause To Stand', K'aŋǧí 'Crow', P'ejí Iyáp'a
'Strikes Grass', and P'ejí Akáŋ Nájiŋ 'Stands On Grass' (La-
violette 1944:123); Sioux Valley, Wamdíska 'White Eagle';
Birdtail, Maȟpíyaduta 'Red Cloud' and Maȟpíya Hináp'e 'Cloud
Appears', also known as Enoch; Oak Lake, Hdémani 'Rattles
Walking' and Íŋkpaduta 'Red Point' (as deer antlers red with
blood); Standing Buffalo, T'at'áŋka Nájiŋ 'Standing Buffalo
Bull'; White Cap or Moose Woods, Wap'áhaska 'White Warbonnet';

Round Plain or Sioux Wahpeton, Mníkapsica 'Splashing Water'
and Íŋkpaduta 'Red Point'; Wood Mountain, T'at'áŋka Íyotake
'Sitting Buffalo Bull'.

The composition of the reserve communities as to bands is
as follows: Sioux Village, mostly Wahpetons, according to Laviolette (1944:114) of the Dwellers On The Sand sub-band, and
probably some Sissetons and others; Sioux Valley, Sissetons in
the majority, with several Mdewakantons and a few Wahpekutes
and Wahpetons; Birdtail, mostly Wahpetons, according to Laviolette (1944:114), but my informants reported a preponder-
ance of Mdewakantons with a few Yanktonais; Oak Lake, mostly
Wahpekutes, some Wahpetons, and according to Laviolette (1944:
123) a few Yanktonais of the P'ábaksa 'Cut Head' sub-band;
Standing Buffalo, mostly Sissetons with a few Wahpetons and
Wahpekutes; White Cap, Sissetons of the C'aŋk'úte sub-band
(cf. Laviolette 1944:119); Round Plain or Sioux Wahpeton,
mostly Wahpetons, with a few of each of the other three Santee
bands; Wood Mountain, mostly Hunkpapa Tetons, with a few
Santees.

3. THE SIOUX IN CANADA

In this chapter I will trace briefly the history of the Sioux since their arrival in Canada and suggest how some of the changes so apparent in present day Canadian Sioux culture have come about. In this historical review I rely heavily on La-violette (1944) and Meyer (1967, 1968).

Of the approximately 6,300 Eastern Sioux who had lived in Minnesota and adjacent portions of North and South Dakota, Iowa, and Wisconsin prior to the Uprising of 1862, fewer than 2,000 were accounted for at the end of the hostilities. Some eight hundred Mdewakantons and Wahpekutes and nearly all of the Sissetons and Wahpetons had fled to the prairies of Dakota Territory, where pursuit by United States troops that autumn was impracticable (Meyer 1968:13). In addition to those who later surrendered or died in the campaign of 1863-1864, some 3,000 eventually settled on the Sisseton and Devil's Lake re-servations in Dakota Territory or on the Fort Peck Reservation in Montana.

The remainder, after drifting back and forth across the border, finally settled in British Territory. Here they were eventually granted tracts of land. Politically, if not cul-turally, these Sioux severed their ties with their relatives in the United States and became a separate entity, the Canadi-an Sioux. Retaining much of their common Sioux heritage, they nevertheless acquired from their contacts with French, Eng-lish, Scotch, Ukranian, and other Euro-Canadians, as well as native Canadian Indian tribes, many additional cultural fea-tures that have made them what they are today.

At the time of the Minnesota Uprising, the principal set-tlement in the Canadian Prairies was at Fort Garry, the Red

River settlement, which became modern Winnipeg, Manitoba.
News of the Minnesota Uprising did not reach Fort Garry until nearly three weeks after it had begun. From that time until the first parties of refugee Sioux arrived in late December 1862, the population of the fort was in a state of nervous
expectation (Meyer 1968:13). The Eastern Sioux, particularly
the "Upper Council" Sissetons and Wahpetons, were not complete
strangers to the residents of Fort Garry. Since 1821 they had
occasionally appeared in the Red River settlement to trade
furs and pemican for English strouds and tobacco, and had always professed friendship for the S̪agdás̪a (British), a friendship based upon military services to the British in the French
and Indian Wars, the American Revolution, and the War of 1812.
Nevertheless, the settlers were apprehensive, as they were
comparatively defenseless and were inclined, as whites, to
believe the most extreme reports of Indian atrocities committed in the Minnesota Valley.

The first Sioux refugees, a group of eighty-six, appeared
at Fort Garry on December 28, 1862. They were without ammunition and were hungry. Their clothes were in rags. This pa-
thetic little party was lodged in the courtroom, the only
place available for their accomodation. None of these, apparently, had been involved in the uprising and only fifteen were
Mdewakantons or Wahpekutes, the two bands principally involved
in the outbreak. After receiving presents of pemican and
other food, the Sioux returned to Devil's Lake on December 31
(Laviolette 1944:50).

In May 1863 a party of about eighty Sioux, including a few
women, arrived at Fort Garry. Headed by Little Crow, the
leader of the Minnesota Uprising, they asked for an interview
with the authorities. The request was granted. Little Crow
displayed British medals and flags that he and his men had in-

herited from their fathers. He said that the elders of the
tribe had been told during the War of 1812 that if they ever
got into trouble with the Americans they should appeal to the
British, and the "folds of the red flag in the north would
wrap them round and preserve them from their enemies" (quoted
in Meyer 1968:14). Little Crow asked Alexander G. Dallas,
Governor of Rupert's Land, to intercede with Gen. Henry H.
Sibley, commander of U.S. forces in Minnesota, in the matter
of prisoners. He also asked that he and his people be allowed
to settle north of the border and that they be given provisions and ammunition. Dallas refused the request for ammunition, but since the Sioux were evidently starving, gave them
some provisions.

Once again the Sioux left, and no more refugees were seen
at Fort Garry until November 20, 1863, when a small party
arrived, followed by a much larger group on December 11. More
continued to arrive until about six hundred Sioux were camped
at Sturgeon Creek, some six miles west of the fort. They were
in a state of extreme destitution, and although many of them
were believed to have been implicated in the atrocities of the
uprising, they were aided from both public and private sources
(Meyer 1968:14).

The usually proud and imperious Santees at this point were
absolutely destitute, reduced to begging from house to house.
The Canadian settlers, who themselves had scarcely enough
food, viewed the mendicant Indians with disgust and fear. So
desperate were the Sioux that some actually sold their children to Canadian farmers (Meyer 1968:15).

Governor Dallas, in an attempt to aid the Sioux, as well as
to remove them from the vicinity of the fort, offered them
food, clothing, and even a supply of ammunition if they would
go to a place where they could hunt and fish. At first re-

luctant, the Sioux finally moved to White Horse Plain, about twenty-five miles up the Assiniboine River, west of Fort Garry. From here they split up into small bands to hunt and fish, some going to Lake Manitoba where they made a good catch of northern pike.

Urged by both Canadian and American authorities to surrender, a few gave themselves up to Maj. Edwin A.C. Hatch, who had been placed in command of a special battalion stationed at Pembina, near the international boundary. Those who surrendered returned to an uncertain fate. Feelings against the Santees still ran high in the United States. In fact two of the Sioux refugees, Chief Shakopee (Šákpe 'Six') and Medicine Bottle (T'áte Ic'ásna Máni 'Wind Rustling Walker'), were taken across the border by United States agents after being subdued with alcohol and chloroform, and were subsequently executed (Meyer 1968:15, Woolworth 1969).

The next spring the Sioux joined the Métis, the Plains Ojibwa mixed bloods with whom they had concluded a treaty in 1862, on their annual buffalo hunt. In late August they returned, together with kinsmen they had met along the way, and now nearly 3,000 Sioux descended on the Red River Settlement. They were again destitute and starving as a result of the destruction of their supplies by Gen. Alfred Sully's force at the battle of Killdeer Mountain earlier that month. William Mactavish, who had succeeded Dallas as governor of Rupert's Land, met them at Portage La Prairie and tried to detain them there, but Standing Buffalo, Waanatan, Leaf, and Turning Thunder, accompanied by a large retinue, insisted on going to Fort Garry. Like those who had been there the previous winter, they begged for food but committed no depredations (Meyer 1968:15).

These Sioux chiefs displayed British flags and medals, as Little Crow had done, and reminded the governor of the promise of assistance given their fathers. Mactavish, however, refused them any help. At this the party became desperate, seizing whatever they could lay their hands on, invading farmers' fields to steal standing crops, and returning at night to run off livestock. Some returned to farms where they had sold children the previous winter and reclaimed them (Meyer 1968: 16).

From this time on the Sioux tended to congregate at Portage La Prairie, Poplar Point, and High Bluff rather than at Fort Garry. During the summer of 1865 some 680 lodges of Sioux were scattered west of the fort. Their situation remained precarious and they were reported to be living on roots, duck eggs, and birds. Trouble with their traditional tribal enemies, the Plains Ojibwas, added to their difficulties. The Plains Ojibwas claimed the area as their own and regarded the Sioux as intruders. In May 1864 a group of Plains Ojibwa warriors fired into the tents of a Sioux fishing camp on Lake Manitoba, killing twenty. Again in June 1866, Standing Buffalo and part of his band, on their return from a visit to Fort Garry, were attacked by Plains Ojibwas. Four men were killed and the white settlers feared that a tribal war would erupt. The Sioux chiefs, however, were aware that any hostilities on their part would result in their quick expulsion from British territory, and they managed to keep their warriors in check.

Meanwhile, in the United States, efforts were being made to restore peace with the Sioux. In 1867 the commanding officer of the District of Minnesota sent a representative to treat with the Canadian refugees. The Sioux were promised complete amnesty and absolution for all past offenses if they would surrender themselves at Fort Abercrombie, a post south of pre-

sent Fargo, North Dakota. All efforts failed, however. Perhaps the Sioux had heard too many false promises from the
great father in Washington, or perhaps the cowardly abduction
and subsequent execution of Six and Medicine Bottle made them
doubt their fate if they crossed the international boundary.

The Sioux of this period were working out a modus vivendi
with the local white settlers, Métis, and Indians. Many Sioux
men found employment as laborers, farm workers, rail-split-
ters, and harvest hands. Others eked out a living in the traditional occupations of fishing, hunting, and trapping. The
women of the tribe earned money as domestics and by taking in
laundry from white families. These contacts with Euro-Canadian settlers were extremely important acculturative experiences
for the Sioux since most such employment was on an individual
or small group basis, and the Sioux took their meals with
their employers. It was apparently at this time that a treaty
with the Plains Ojibwas took place. This ended the continual
worry that small parties of Sioux hunters or fishermen would
be attacked by Plains Ojibwas as occurred in 1864 and 1866.
By December 1869 there were five hundred Sioux wintering at
Portage La Prairie, including a group recently arrived from
the Souris River, near the international boundary. Still more
came in 1870 (Meyer 1968:17).

In 1870 the Hudson's Bay Company's territorial holdings
were transferred to the new Dominion of Canada, and the Province of Manitoba was created. By Treaties 1 and 2 the native
Swampy Crees and Plains Ojibwas ceded their lands to the
Crown. A few months later, Wemyss M. Simpson, who had negotiated these treaties, called attention to the presence of the
Sioux in Manitoba. He wrote, "Since their appearance in British territory they have, on all occasions, conducted themselves in a quiet and orderly manner, and although they ack-

nowledge the fact of their having no claims upon Her Majesty, they look with hope to her benevolence in their endeavors to live in peace and quiet within her possessions." Although the Sioux were not "Treaty Indians," Simpson argued that they should not be left uncared for in the face of a growing scarcity of game that might "reduce them to a starving and therefore desperate condition" (Meyer 1968:17).

There were no immediate results, but finally in 1873 a reserve of twelve thousand acres was authorized for the Sioux on the Little Saskatchewan (Minnedosa) River. However, the Sioux rejected this site, asking for two or three smaller reserves instead. The two new sites were (1) on the Assiniboine River at the mouth of Oak River (for many years thereafter called Oak River Reserve, but now called Sioux Valley) and (2) near the Hudson's Bay Company post of Fort Ellice, at the junction of Birdtail Creek with the Assiniboine River (present Birdtail Reserve). For several years, however, the bulk of the Sioux refused to settle on reserves, preferring to winter at Portage or in the Turtle Mountains near the international boundary.

There was also a considerable band of Eastern Sioux under White Cap and the son of Standing Buffalo who ranged further west on the Qu'Appelle River in present Saskatchewan. When contacted by treaty commissioners in 1875, White Cap informed them that his people had been in the region for thirteen years and that they wished to be left as they were, with the privilege of hunting with the Métis. They did not want to settle on reserves with the other Sioux (Meyer 1968:19).

Even those who desired to locate permanently were not all accommodated by the two reserves established in 1875. There were a number of Wahpekutes living in the vicinity of the Turtle Mountains. A reserve four miles square was created for them in 1877 near Oak Lake (present Oak Lake Reserve). Part

of the band refused to settle there, however, so another reserve of a single square mile was established for them about
1883 on the north slope of the Turtle Mountains (Meyer 1968:
19). This reserve is no longer in existence.

Meanwhile the Standing Buffalo and White Cap bands, which
separated from one another in 1874, refused to settle on the
reserves. They were given agricultural implements and seed
potatoes in 1877 and told to plant at Qu'Appelle Lakes. When
a single reserve was proposed for them, the two chiefs quar-
reled. The impasse was resolved by establishing two reserves,
one at Qu'Appelle Lakes (present Standing Buffalo Reserve),
the other at Moose Woods on the South Saskatchewan River about
eighteen miles south of Saskatoon (present White Cap Reserve).
These were surveyed in 1880 and 1881.

Neither band was anxious to settle down, however, and many
of these Sioux ranged north to Prince Albert and southwest to
the Cypress Hills. Those who remained on the reserves had a
difficult time, and in May 1881 when an agent arrived at White
Cap he reported that the people were destitute. He helped
them plant a small crop and build eight houses (Meyer 1968:
20).

The Canadian Sioux gradually acquired a status essentially
similar to that of the native "Treaty Indians," but government
administration was very haphazard at first. In 1878 an agent
was appointed for the three Manitoba bands, but Standing Buffalo Reserve was allowed to shift for itself until the mid-
1880s. Not until 1882 was a farming instructor or "boss farmer" hired for White Cap's band.

Several Sioux assigned to White Cap Reserve spent much of
their time in and near Prince Albert, Saskatchewan, where seasonal jobs were available, and as early as 1880 a farming instructor was assigned to look after destitute Indians in the

area. By 1891 a Presbyterian school was opened for these
Sioux, and in 1894 a reserve consisting of a block of four
sections was established northwest of Prince Albert (present
Round Plain or Sioux Wahpeton Reserve). In 1908 two more sections were added in an effort to make the locale more attrac-
tive for settlement.

Another reserve created in the 1890s was Sioux Village, a
belated recognition of the Sioux community that had been in
Canada longer than any other. This reserve is extremely interesting from a sociological point of view since from its in-
ception it has been urban in nature. The Sioux at Sioux Village were individuals who had not gone to Birdtail or Oak
River but had lingered in the Portage area. About 1886, local
white citizens established a school for these people and encouraged them to save money to purchase a tract of land. When
they had accumulated $400 they purchased twenty-six acres on
the Assiniboine River within the limits of the town. The
Presbyterian church built a chapel for them on this land and
a non-reserve "Sioux village" developed. Its occupants supported themselves as laborers in Portage or as farmhands in
the surrounding area. In 1898 the Canadian government gave
this group a 109 acre lot in a location less subject to spring
flooding. This they subsequently exchanged for a twenty-five
acre lot just west of town (present Sioux Village Reserve).
Most of the community still lives there today and refused to
move even when, in 1934, the government purchased a much larger tract for them adjacent to Long Plain Reserve, a Plains
Ojibwa reserve a few miles to the southwest (Meyer 1968:25).

The final Sioux reserve in Canada, Wood Mountain, was established in 1913. Sitting Bull and some of his people had
camped in the Wood Mountain area, southwest of present Moose
Jaw, Saskatchewan, off and on for many years. After the Bat-

tle of the Little Big Horn in 1876, pressed on all sides by
United States military units, Sitting Bull decided to lead his
people to Canada. He is reported to have confided to a Métis
scout named La Framboise:

> We can find peace in the land of the Grandmoth-
> er. We can sleep sound there, our women and chil-
> dren can lie down and feel safe. I don't under-
> stand why the Red Coats gave us and our country to
> the Americans. We are the Grandmother's children
> and when we go across the Medicine Road (the bound-
> ary) we shall bury the hatchet. My own grandfath-
> er told me the Red Coats were our people and good
> people and I must always trust them as friends.
> [Laviolette 1944:86]

In May 1877, Sitting Bull and his uncle Four Horns, with
135 lodges, crossed the line into Canada. Other Tetons under
Black Moon were already camped at Wood Mountain and Sitting
Bull and his people joined them. Both Canadian and U.S. officials were uneasy about such a large force of warriors so near
the international boundary, fearing that they might suddenly
recross and strike Gen. Nelson A. Miles' forces. On October
15, with the assistance of the Northwest Mounted Police, Gen.
Alfred H. Terry and A.G. Lawrence met with Sitting Bull at
Fort Walsh and attempted to induce him to return to the United
States. Sitting Bull and the other chiefs emphatically refused to leave, Sitting Bull telling Terry:

> You are a bigger fool than I am if you think I
> believe you. This place, the home of the soldiers
> of the Grandmother, is the Medicine House where
> the truth lives and you come here to tell us lies.
> When you go back to your country, take your lies
> with you. [Laviolette 1944:93]

The American government insisted that the Canadian government should either compel the refugees to return or oblige them to withdraw a greater distance from the international boundary. However, the Canadian authorities refused to take either course so long as the refugee Tetons refrained from hostile or lawless acts.

Finally, it was starvation that brought about the return of Sitting Bull and the bulk of his people to the United States in 1881. Only Brown Eagle and a few of his followers remained in Canada, with about one hundred and fifty lodges. This number gradually dwindled, for as the years went by, family after family returned to join their relatives on the Standing Rock Reservation in North and South Dakota. Today only seventy Sioux live on Wood Mountain Reserve.

4. TRADITIONAL HISTORY

The mythologies and folktales of a people often reveal many things about that group not intended by the story teller. As E. B. Tylor, the eminent nineteenth century British anthropologist remarked, "Were nothing to be had out of ancient poetry except distorted memories of historical events, the anthropologist might be wise to set it aside altogether. Yet, looked at from another point of view, it is one of his most perfect and exact sources of knowledge" (Tylor 1930:113). What Tylor refers to is the inclusion in myths and legends of bits of detail telling us not only of former customs, long abandoned in a culture, as well as more recent accretions demonstrating how the culture has changed.

The Canadian Sioux, who possess a lively historical tradition, are no exception to the general rule, and in the little more than a century that they have dwelt on Canadian soil have begun to develop in their oral tradition interesting accounts of how they came to be there and the events that led up to their exodus from the United States. These accounts, although they may depart from documented historical fact, are quite revealing as to how the Sioux themselves interpret and remember these events. In 1972 I recorded two excellent traditional histories at Birdtail Reserve, one from Simon Hanska (Mdewakanton band, age 73) and George Bear (Yanktonai band, age 93). Both men are held in high repute as tribal historians not only on their own reserve, but also at Sioux Valley. As is common with historians in many cultures, each has little regard for the other as a historian. The two accounts are presented here as representative examples of oral history and should be taken as such, not judged by the standards of academic historians.

Simon Hanska's Account

The Dakota originated in the east. The earliest place mentioned is Psiŋhú Wakpá 'Wild Rice River'. This must be the Saint Lawrence River in the area of the present Quebec City. They were there four or five hundred years ago. When they were there they met the Sagdása [English]. The English fought the French at that time and the Sioux helped the English. After this the Sioux came on the south side of the river. They came to a place called Two Mountains, in the present state of Ohio. From here they came to Nice Bank where they were neighbors of the Hot'áŋke (Winnebagos). Then they came north of Miracle Valley to Wiyáka Ot'ína 'Dwellers On The Sand'. From there they came to Minnesota.

In 1850 [1851] they negotiated their first treaty with the United States. They negotiated nine treaties in all, each time giving up more land. They were supposed to get money (annuities) from this but they did not. This led to the Minnesota Uprising. In 1864 they came to Winnipeg and asked the officials for permission to stay. As proof of their old friendship with the English they showed the officials old British medals and flags. The Canadian officials were surprised to see these. Governor Morris said, "You can stay. We will buy land from the Cree [Plains Ojibwas] for you." At first they settled near Portage but in 1864 they left and walked to Griswold [Sioux Valley]. They came here, to Birdtail Reserve, in 1875.

The Wild Rice River of Mr. Hanska's account may perhaps be intended for the river of that name in Minnesota, a tributary of the Red River of the North, which rises in Clearwater County, Minnesota, and flows through Mahnomen and Norman counties. There is no historical material that would support a location of the Sioux on the St. Lawrence River. Nor is there historical evidence that any substantial number of Eastern Sioux took part in the French and Indian Wars, although many were active on the British side in the War of 1812. Wiyaka Otina, given in this account as a placename, is the name of one of the Wahpeton bands listed by Ashley (Riggs 1893:158). By the treaty of 1851 the Santees transferred to the United States all their lands in Iowa, the Dakotas, and Minnesota except for a tract on the upper Minnesota River which they reserved for their future occupancy. The English medals and flags owned by the Santees in the mid-nineteenth century may have been those distributed to chiefs and headmen at a general council in Montreal on August 18, 1778, to recognize the assistance the Santees rendered to British troops in the Kentucky and Illinois campaigns during the American Revolution (Laviolette 1944:22).

George Bear's Account

The first time the Dakota saw white men they shook hands with them. One of the white men had a musket and fired it. This scared the Dakota and they all ran away. These white men were English. Later these whites and the Dakota made a treaty and the English gave silver medals and a flag to the Dakota. My family still has one of these medals with the image of George III on it. The flags are now all lost, but I saw one in 1922. At this time the Dakota lived in the east. Shortly

after this they began to move west. When they came
to Arizona [sic] they met a young boy with supernatural powers. He told them he would bring meat,
and turned toward the woods and shot an arrow.
The Dakota went in the direction he had fired and
found a dead "jumper" (whitetail deer). This boy
stayed with the Dakota many years, and grew to
adulthood and old age. Finally, when he was very
old, he told the people he was going to die and
that they should bury him in a certain place. They
did as he instructed. From his grave a strange new
plant grew. It was corn. I think that this man
was Hiawatha, but I never heard his Dakota name.

I secured my Dakota history from Sioux Ben, a
great Sioux warrior, a member of the Wahpeton.
Originally the Dakota lived in the east. They
were at a narrow place south of New York. They
traveled along the seashore and arrived at a big
mountain. A river flowed from this mountain and
the Dakota decided to follow it. It took them
west. As they traveled they sent out an advance
party. These scouts came back and said, "We have
found a good country." This was Minnesota. The
Dakota came and settled there. They lived there
many years, but finally the whites came and settled
all around them. Finally they sold most of their
lands to these whites. In 1862 they were starving.
The traders refused to extend any credit. One
trader [Andrew J. Myrick] said, "Go home and eat
grass." Finally they rose against the whites.
When they did so they killed this trader and stuffed his mouth with grass [cf. Laviolette 1944:35].

They fought the soldiers but were defeated. They
fled from Minnesota to Canada in 1862. They entered Canada east of Grand Forks, North Dakota. This
was in the c'aŋpásapa wí, 'black cherries moon'
(August). It was a terrible time. Old people were
abandoned and killed. Babies were killed. Both
the Dakota and whites committed atrocities.

During the battles the women and children would
hide in the grass. The Dakota managed to kill
eight hundred settlers but finally lost the war.

Near Grand Forks they made bullboats and crossed
the Red River. From here they went north across
the border southwest of Winnipeg. In order to hunt
and protect themselves from the Saulteaux [Plains
Ojibwas] they tried to purchase percussion caps and
balls for their guns, but the Canadians refused to
sell. They tried a second time and secured some.

The Saulteaux were after them, so they kept moving. They stopped near Portage for a while. They
carried burning brands from one camp to another to
keep warm. Some stopped at Portage. Others went
to Turtle Mountain. On this trip my grandfather
carried ten bags of shot, each weighing ten pounds.
He later died from his exertions. Next they moved
to Griswold (Sioux Valley).

Enemies were all around. The Crees and Assiniboines joined together against us. Finally the
government gave us protection. Since there wasn't
enough game the chiefs decided to split up.
Hdémani 'Rattles Walking' and Íŋkpaduta 'Scarlet
Point' went to Pipestone. Mahpíya Hináp'a 'Cloud
Appears', also called Enoch, and his people came

here. T'at'áŋka Nájiŋ 'Standing Buffalo' went to
Fort Qu'Appelle. Wap'áhaska 'White Warbonnet'
went to Saskatoon.

Jim Kiyewakan, of the Basswood Legging String band of the
Sissetons/Wahpetons, and Wahpekutes, related the following
graphic account of the flight of one group of Sioux from Minnesota.

Jim Kiyewakan's Account

In 1862 the Santee were in their village when
a messenger arrived. He said, "The Isáŋt'aŋka
'Long Knives' [American soldiers] are coming. You
had better run away!" They fled, leaving most of
their worldly goods. Tents, travois, and beautiful painted parfleches were abandoned. Even
babies were abandoned in the confusion, and some
were trampled to death. People were singing medicine songs to secure help from the supernatural.

They fled until they came to the Mississippi
River. Here they constructed bullboats to transport the children across. The adults swam, holding on to horses' tails.

A steamboat came by as they were crossing and
began firing at the refugees with a cannon. The
Dakota knew about steamboats, so the warriors began to fire at the wheelman and succeeded in killing him. With the wheelman dead the boat drifted
and lodged on a sand bar. The Dakota then killed
the soldiers and crew and looted the boat. They
found gold coins and some of the young men skipped
them over the surface of the water as a contest,
much as one skips a flat stone. They also found
bundles of paper money and tore them open. Some

of the bills flew up, in the wind, and lodged in tree branches. It must have been an army payroll.

From this place they fled west to C'edí Ojú 'Reed-like-grass Planting' [Poplar, Montana]. While there the women busied themselves washing buffalo guts in the Missouri River to make t'aní-ġa, tripe soup. While they were busy word came to them that t'óka 'enemies' were coming.

They fled again and went west from there. From a point south of Medicine Hat they crossed the border into Canada. They lived in this vicinity for two or three years. Then they came to Regina and stayed six or seven years. Then they went to the vicinity of Duck Lake, Saskatchewan. They were here in 1885 when the Frenchmen [Métis] asked them to join in their rebellion. Some Sioux went to help the Frenchmen. My mother was a part of a group of Dakota who assisted these Frenchmen. She cooked for the Frenchmen soldiers. She said it was a curious thing--both sides would stop shooting when it was mealtime. Many Indians of different tribes were on their way to join the Frenchmen but the war ended before they could join it. The P'óge Hdóka (Nez Perce) were one tribe that came to help.

From here the Dakota went to Prince Albert, then to Saskatoon, then to Fort Qu'Appelle, and finally they came here. My mother was born west of Pleasant Lake. My father heard about the Minnesota Uprising. He didn't see it. He was afraid, so he came north to Winnipeg to avoid trouble.

Mr. Kiyewakan's account illuminates the movements of
those Sioux who traveled west before turning north and crossing into Canada. From other sources we know that this group
numbered some four hundred individuals. A larger group, num-
bering perhaps six hundred, moved directly from Minnesota and
eastern North and South Dakota into present Manitoba, then
called Red River Colony. Frank Merrick, a man of mixed Sioux
and white descent who lives on the Long Plain Reserve, gave a
traditional historical account of the movements of this group.
Mr. Merrick, who was 87 years old in 1972, is a well-known
figure in Manitoba, and until illness forced him to curtail
such activities, he was often called upon to represent Canadian Indians at state ceremonies in Winnipeg.

Frank Merrick's Account

The Sioux who settled here came from the States
originally. They came to Sioux Lookout first, then
moved to Poplar Point. Here they were attacked by
Saulteaux [Plains Ojibwas]. They moved to Free
Island, where they were attacked again. Then they
moved to South Portage. I was born there. People
set aside land for them near Sioux Village, but
the ice cut away most of the land. Finally the
government bought them lots at their present location [Sioux Village], twenty acres in extent, and
erected twenty houses for them.

There was a lot of trouble between the Sioux and
the Saulteaux near Portage in the early days. The
Sioux realized that unless they could make peace
they would be wiped out. Finally twenty Sioux men
dressed for war and marched into the Bungi [Plains
Ojibwa] camp. As they marched they sang this song:

Oyáte kiŋ waŋmáyaka po.
Até t'ac'áŋnuŋpa yuhá mawáni.

You tribes watch me!
I walk carrying my father's pipe.

They asked for a council and wanted to smoke. The
Bungi agreed, all except for one man. The chief
said, "You will be dead by sundown (unless you
agree)." Finally he agreed as well. The two
tribes, Sioux and Saulteaux, danced together for
two days [to cement the peace treaty].

Later the Bungi returned the visit. As they
entered the Sioux camp they sang:

Kanawa pamɩsik nondawɩsik.
Nimaca pimatiasa noga osɩk.

All you people listen to me.
I am prepared to fight.

Again the two tribes, Bungi and Sioux, danced together for two days. They have been at peace
ever since.

Among the Santees who came to Canada were both leaders and
participants in the Minnesota Uprising as well as members of
the peace party. The latter group included most of the Sissetons and Wahpetons, who fled to the "Grandmother's Land" because they felt (correctly) that they would be implicated regardless of their non-participation in hostilities. At first
there was undoubtedly some bad feeling between the hostiles
and the peace party, but their common tribulations soon re-
united them. In 1972 I could find no trace of rancor toward
Little Crow or other leaders of the hostiles. Mrs. Arthur
Young of Oak Lake Reserve is a descendant of Chief Inkpaduta,

a niece of his granddaughter Waŋbdíhotewiŋ 'Gray Eagle Woman'.
Although Inkpaduta is portrayed in histories as a renegade
hated by whites and repudiated by his own people as well, Mrs.
Young seemed unaware of his negative historical image. She
was proud to claim relationship with him, commenting, "If he
was a bad man, you can bet it was white men who pushed him to
his bad deeds."

Many older Canadian Sioux still remember the intense poverty of the early years after their flight from the U.S. In
place of their comfortable log or frame farm houses they had
to live in canvas tipis the year round. Recalling these early
years, Emma Pratt (Mdewakanton and Sisseton, age 88, Sioux
Valley) commented that there was no tipi in the village that
was not patched and repatched. All sorts of food was eaten
to sustain life. She remembered that her aunt used to trap
mice in a container of bear grease (used because it does not
harden). The mice were skinned and cooked, but even though
the children were hungry, they refused to eat them. Muskrats
were often eaten as well.

Martha Tawiyaka (Sisseton, age 88, Standing Buffalo) recalled highlights of her long life among the Saskatchewan Santees.

Martha Tawiyaka's Account

I was four years old at the time of the second
Northwest Uprising. My grandpa and grandma were
there. The Sioux and Cree were enemies. I was
playing outside one day in March. My mother said,
"Come in or the t'óka ['enemy', the Crees] will
get you." We saw a man on a hill and were afraid
it was an enemy. It was only my grandpa. He had
run away on foot from Duck Lake to avoid being involved in the war. My aunt cried and then started

to cook. Soon the rest of the family came in a
Red River cart.

I can remember the Mounties and the soldiers
when they were camped at Fort Qu'Appelle before the
march to Duck Lake.

A S̊ahíe [Cree] was the one who started the war.
He was named Almighty Voice. He was going to kill
three cows to feed his starving people. Some of
the Sioux were forced to join the Cree. Some of
them fled here to avoid being involved, some fled
to Fort Totten [North Dakota] and some to Griswold
[Sioux Valley].

I went to school at Lebret when I was seven. I
stayed there twelve years. I liked it there with
the sisters. One time they took me with them to
Winnipeg to a religious retreat. No one was allowed to speak. I liked it. I decided that I wanted
to be a Gray Nun, but my father came and took me
out of school when he heard of this.

The Evangelical Church came here eight years
ago (1964). I was a strong Roman Catholic before
that, but my daughter put me in that [Evangelical]
church. I used to be a great dancer, too, before
my husband died. I had good medicine, too. But
when I joined the Evangelical Church I dug a big
hole and buried all my medicines and said, "No
more Indian ways! I'd rather follow Jesus!" In
1967 I was sick and nearly died of a gallstone.
My husband was an Indian doctor. He blew on people
[to cure them]. I was a midwife and I made good
medicine.

I used to see the Wak'áŋ Wac'ípi 'Medicine

Dance'. I saw it four different times. One time
the [Catholic] priest saw some of us girls there
and scolded us. My mother belonged to the Wak'án
Wac'ípi.

My grandsons farm all around here. I used to
do washing to earn cash money. I would start at
6:00 a.m. and walk to town [a distance of about
ten miles]. I would work all day for white people,
washing clothes. At 4:00 my husband would hitch
up the team and come and get me.

If you ask me what is most different about
young people today and young people when I grew up
I would say this: Today's young people have no
respect.

My grandma used to talk about C'aŋót'ina
['Little Tree Dweller'].

I can speak Cree and French. I learned French
from the Gray Nuns and Cree from Cree girls at
Lebret.

At an early age I learned to tan hides and to
sew with sinew. I can make porcupine quillwork,
too.

I like to eat porcupine. To cook porcupine you
boil it a few minutes first, then bake it. I still
dry venison and make wasná [pemican]. I never eat
garlic, bologna, eggs, or store-bought bread. I
eat venison, duck, and rabbit. Duck eggs are good.
I make buns. I never drink coffee, only tea.

I like it here [Standing Buffalo Reserve]. The
Sioux up here are neat and keep their yards clean.
In the States they have trash piles right outside
of the door. Some houses have doors that are
greasy.

I am afraid of snakes.

Swan meat is not good to eat. It is too fishy tasting, but crane tastes good.

The lake here used to be clear and sweet smelling the year around. Now it is green and smells bad all summer. We used to drink from the lake when I was young.

One year at the Regina fair I saw the Heyoka [Thunder dreamers]. They embarassed me by calling me "mother." My maternal grandfather used to be a Heyoka. He had a medicine they used to prevent being burned or scalded. They used to punish people at dances by making them dip into a boiling kettle to get meat. He could do this without getting scalded. He gave this medicine to my uncle and he did the same thing.

My late husband was a Thunder dreamer. He used to fill a pipe before a storm and ask the Thunder to come quietly. He also smudged with sweetgrass for the same purpose. Sometimes he would cry [to make himself pitiable in the eyes of the Thunderbirds]. Before a fierce storm the Thunders would shout "Wuwoo!" to let him know lightning was going to strike.

Sitting Bull put on a Ghost Dance [?] when he and his band were camped here. We girls went to see it. During the day they danced powwow. At night they wore white clothing, masks, and looked like ghosts.

We used to use buffalo ribs as knives and we had wooden plates and spoons.

Mrs. Tawiyaka's account is confusing in reference to the Ghost
Dance. Sitting Bull's visit to Fort Qu'Appelle took place in
June 1881, many years before the Sioux adopted the Ghost
Dance. As far as is known, the only full-scale performance of
the original Ghost Dance in Canada took place in 1895 at a
fork of the Wood River, six miles northwest of Gravelbourg,
Saskatchewan (Laviolette 1944:19). Furthermore, masks were
never a part of Ghost Dance regalia.

Of all the Canadian Sioux, only those at the tiny Wood
Mountain Reserve are Tetons. They came to Canada in May 1877,
and most subsequently returned to the U.S. A few remained
under the leadership of Brown Eagle and Black Bull. Today
they are proud of their distinctive background. Pete Lethbridge, long a leader on this reserve, provided a brief account of their history.

Pete Lethbridge's Account

I am a half-breed, half English and half Sioux.
My mother is Hunkpapa, Sitting Bull's band. We
came up here after the Little Big Horn fight. We
were at Willow Bunch, then we came up here. In
the Riel Uprising they [the Métis] talked my people
into joining [with them]. Red Bear, one of my
grandfathers, was killed in battle. He was shot
in the leg and died of the wound. Another grandfather was captured and died in prison.

We are T'ít'uŋwaŋ, the only real Sioux in Canada. We speak the "L" dialect.

My mother was in the camp at the Battle of the
Little Big Horn. She was nine years old at the
time. She remembers one young man, a crazy boy,
who stripped Custer's uniform from his body and
put it on. He also had a bugle he picked up on

the battlefield. He got on his horse and paraded around, but when he blew the bugle his horse bucked him off.

After moving to Canada, the Sioux fought briefly with the
Plains Ojibwas. Probably during those early years the formal
war organization, including the war chief and soldier lodge,
was activated as it had been during earlier times in Minnesota. But the imposition of peace among the tribes by the Canadian government made warfare a part of the Sioux past rather
than an ongoing aspect of their lives. Still, Canadian Sioux
today recall traditions relating to warfare.

According to Robert Good Voice, before going off on an expedition the warriors would dance the Suŋkáh Wac'ípi 'Dog
Imitators Dance'. In this dance the livers of dogs, killed on
the spot, were removed, cut into strips, and hung on the top
of a pole about five feet tall. The warriors danced around
this pole, acting like hungry dogs. Finally one of the warriors grabbed a piece of the liver in his teeth and swallowed
it. Others followed suit until all of the raw liver had been
consumed. None but a shaman was allowed to touch the liver
with his hands. The dance lasted all night. Afterward, those
warriors going on the expedition retired some distance from
the village and prepared for war. Mr. Good Voice recalled one
of the songs of this dance, the words of which might be translated:

> The one I love is going to war,
> The one I hate is going to stay home.

This song, like those of many of the social dances, supposedly
expresses the feelings of one of the young women of the village.

A Santee warrior went into battle naked except for breechcloth, leggings, and moccasins. His weapons were a ball-head

or rabbit-leg warclub (later replaced by trade tomahawks), a
bow and about twenty arrows, and a scalping knife. Later, the
bow and arrows were replaced or supplemented by musket and
ball. Some warriors also carried circular shields made from
the neck of a bison bull, treated by a process of heating and
shrinking until it was slightly convex and about one-half inch
thick. From their use as ceremonial paraphernalia in the nineteenth century we also infer that lances, either straight or
with a crook at the end (to allow the warrior to lean into his
thrust with his shoulder), were used at an early period. By
the time of the flight from Minnesota to Canada, however, such
lances were used only as symbols of men's and women's societies. One such lance, the last one to survive among the Canadian Sioux, was kept by an old man named Jim Mackay. In 1958
I paid a special visit to his home to see this object. It was
of the crooked lance type, about five feet long. When displayed at dances or parades it was wrapped with strips of otter skin and had eagle feathers attached along the shaft at
ten inch intervals.

The Santee war party generally preferred ambush to frontal
attack, firing on the enemy from concealed positions. When
provoked, however, warriors were capable of acts of great
bravery, such as rushing out under fire to retrieve the body
of a fallen comrade. As with other tribes of the Woodlands
and Prairie regions, the Santees awarded their highest acclaim
to that warrior who, in battle, touched an enemy with his
lance, quirt, or some other object held in the hand. This act
was termed iyók'iheya kté 'following the killing' and is commonly translated "counting coup." The enemy could be touched
either alive or dead, although the name for the act would indicate that usually coup was counted upon dead enemies.
Three warriors could count coup on each enemy, first coup

being the most prestigious. Each of these three coups earned the counter the right to wear an eagle feather, according to Kenneth Eastman (Oak Lake). Mr. Eastman did not remember if the eagle feathers earned in this manner were worn in a distinctive fashion, but Landes (1968:211) reported that the feather for the first coup was worn erect, for the second pointing earthward, and for the third the warrior was entitled to wear an "Indian costume," probably the crow belt, a dancing bustle of feathers (cf. Fletcher and LaFlesche 1911:441).

Although no particular honor accrued to the person who did so, the Santee warrior also scalped his fallen enemy when the opportunity afforded. The scalp was cleaned, trimmed, and stretched on a small wooden hoop by the warrior who took it. He presented it to his sister or other female relative on the return of the war party. She then danced with this scalp tied to the end of a long pole, accompanied by other female relatives of the members of the war party. The dance which they performed was termed Iwákici Wac'ípi 'Dance In Praise Of One', usually called the "Victory Dance" or "Scalp Dance." After dancing the scalp, it was buried at some spot away from the village. It was thought that the spirit of the man who was scalped would be the servant of the scalper in the next world. Scalps have not been taken by the Canadian Sioux for a century, but in 1972 I noticed a Grass dancer carrying a replica of a scalp in its drying frame with the legend, "Sioux Village, Portage La Prairie, Manitoba" painted on the hide.

Large war bundles and smaller war medicines (both called wóp'iye, the latter also called wót'awe) were an important part of the equipment of every warrior. The war medicine usually consisted of a small circle of buckskin in which vermillion, minerals, plant substances, hair, animal fur, and the like were wrapped. Usually a man's war bundle related to the

vision that he had received while performing the Vision Quest.
These bundles were larger in size than the war medicines and
were often encased in Woodland type yarn bags. They contained
larger amounts of the same paints, stones, herb medicines (for
treating wounds), animal and bird skins, and sometimes feathers or other charms that the owner--a war leader--could dis-
tribute to members of a war party who were otherwise unpro-
vided. The war bundle of the famous chief Little Crow, seen
in a private museum in Minneapolis in 1960, consisted of a
cylinder of birchbark, the ends of which were notched and
turned in, encasing the complete dried skin of a golden eagle.

According to Kenneth Eastman (Oak Lake), war medicines or
war bundles were made for Canadian Sioux boys who went away to
fight in Europe in World War I. One of these doughboys, Sam
Dowan, was saved from a bayonet wound by his New Testament and
his war medicine, both of which he kept in his left shirt
pocket. The bayonet was stopped by these two items, and although Sam lost an arm, he returned to Manitoba alive.

To the Santees, like other tribal groups throughout the
world, all non-Sioux were t'óka, a word meaning both 'foreign-
ers' and 'enemies'. All non-Sioux were potential enemies. In
their Minnesota homeland the traditional enemies of the Santees were the Hahát'uŋwaŋ 'Dwellers At The Rapids', the Ojibwas (Chippewas). A state of chronic warfare existed between
these people, who had invaded Minnesota from the east, and the
Santees. In spite of this continual conflict there was a
great deal of intermarriage and cultural exchange between the
two tribes.

After their flight to Canada the Sioux encountered new
groups. In the Fort Garry vicinity, during the first years on
Canadian soil, the Santees met and warred with the Plains O-
jibwas, a group that had split off from the Ojibwas proper of

Ontario and Minnesota, and taken to the prairies (cf. Howard
1961, 1965). These people, since they were of Ojibwa origin,
are termed Hahát'uŋwaŋ by the Santees in their own language and
"Saulteaux" in English. Eventually, however, a peace was concluded between the two tribes. Allies of the Plains Ojibwas
were the Saíya (Saíe), Crees and Plains Crees (who are often
confused with the Plains Ojibwas), and the Hóhe, Assiniboines.
The Assiniboines and Sioux share a common origin, but they
were nevertheless bitter enemies right up until the reservation period, and there is still bad blood between the two
tribes.

The Sioux in Canada abandoned their formal war organization. There were probably good reasons for this. For one,
the refugees realized that they were in the "Grandmother's
Land" on the sufferance of Canadian authorities and they
wished to present a peaceable image. For another, they were
in such desperate circumstances that they were not inclined,
as band or village groups, to mount aggressive attacks on anyone. Nevertheless, the position of the warrior still carried
with it great prestige and honor. The warpath still was the
principal path to fame and fortune for the young Sioux man.
The result of all this was an increase in somewhat surrepti-
tious raids, usually initiated by one or two warriors with a
small group of followers, often against the will of the band
chief and council. The purpose of these raids was to secure
horses and other booty and to gain war honors.

Descriptions of Canadian Sioux raiding parties were recorded from informants in 1972. Wallis (1947) provides many more
(also see Landes 1959). A common feature of all such stories
is the enormous weight the Sioux attach to supernatural power.
Examples of two such stories, both from Jim Kiyewakan (Sioux
Valley), are presented here as typical examples.

Once a sixteen year old Dakota youth wanted
to go to war. A party of thirty warriors was plan-
ning to go on a raid and he wished to join them.
His parents, however, would not let him go, as he
was too young. He therefore stole extra pairs of
moccasins and wópapi (pemican) and left anyway.
He had with him only a bow and arrows, a scalping
knife, and a tomahawk. He followed the war party,
starting two hours after they left so that he
would not be noticed. Knowing that they would
send him back if he made his presence known near
the village, he followed them at a distance for
four days and four nights.

Finally, when there was no longer any danger
of his being sent back, he made his presence
known and joined the party. Some of the party
were angry that such a tender youth, who might
hamper their movements, had joined them, but their
leader said, "Maybe he knows something [i.e., has
supernatural power]. Let him stay."

The party continued toward the enemy country.
Finally they came to a desert, where the only
cover was sagebrush. The leader said, "Run, so we
can reach those bushes yonder!" [The Santees,
being Woodland Indians, feared open country, and
the party was afoot.] Again, the leader advised,
"Jump when you cross open places so that enemies,
who may have discovered our trail, cannot follow
our tracks."

The place they had come to was near the Rocky
Mountains. Since there was no timber there in
which to hide, the party hid in a cave during the day.

Scouts were posted outside the cave mouth to watch.
One scout reported back saying that a horseman had
been observed approaching the cave. The leader
advised, "If he sees our tracks, kill him, lest he
give the alarm." The rider passed by, however,
and did not see the tracks.

This lone rider was followed by a large party
of mounted warriors. To the horror of the Dakota
this party dismounted near the cave entrance and
prepared to make camp. It became evident to the
Dakota that sooner or later their presence would
be discovered. Each Dakota warrior therefore prepared for battle and flight by jettisoning all
extra clothing and robes, retaining only his hand
weapons, the clothing he was wearing, and his
wót'awe [personal war medicine packet, the smaller
type of wóp'iye]. The sixteen year old boy was
observed to be trembling with fear, since he did
not have a wót'awe. The leader of the party noticed the boy's trembling and gave him some of his
own wót'awe's contents. Once he had a portion of
the leader's medicine the boy stopped shaking.
Now fully prepared, the group made their attempt
at escape.

They were soon noticed by the enemy, who pursued them and called up more of their tribe. A
party of some five hundred were now in hot pursuit
of the fleeing Dakota. The Dakota stopped and
fought four delaying actions. The last time they
took refuge in a pté mak'ópaza (buffalo wallow).
The enemy braves, who were well mounted, would
ride up to this refuge and shoot as they rode past.

One enemy was gorgeously attired in a fine warbonnet and was riding a kdeskȧ (pinto).

The leader of the Sioux said, "Leave that one
for me!" Taking careful aim he shot the pretty
enemy and took his warbonnet, counting the first
coup. The pinto pony he gave to the sixteen year
old boy. The death of the pretty enemy infuriated
the rest of his people, and several fired at the
Dakota leader. One bullet hit him in the head,
killing him instantly. They also shot another
Dakota in the heel.

These were the only casualties suffered by the
Sioux. When night fell the rest escaped, including the sixteen year old boy with his pinto. I
met that boy years later, when he had become an
old man, in 1917. He had been given the name
Kíciwak'aŋk'aŋ 'Performs Miracles' as a war name
from his deeds on this war party.

Once a party of fifteen Dakota warriors went to
steal horses. They were hiding during the day in
some chokecherry bushes. The enemy discovered them
in their hiding place and launched an attack. Now
it happened that a grizzly bear was in this same
clump of chokecherries, eating the fruit. This
bear chased the enemies away. The enemy thought
that it was a member of the Dakota war party who
had changed himself into a bear. Actually, it
was a magical bear. When the enemy had left the
bear told the Dakota, "I saw that you were in difficulty and wanted to help you. When you return
home you must stage a Wak'áŋ Wóhaŋpi ['Medicine
Feast'] and cook twelve ducks for me. They did
this.

6. ECONOMY

In their new situation in Manitoba and Saskatchewan, the Santees no longer had access to many food sources available in
their Minnesota homeland. Lakes with wild rice were scarce,
and the unsettled conditions following their exodus from the
United States resulted in the near abandonment of gardening by
the Sioux. On the other hand, hunting, fishing, and gathering
wild plants were still possible. Gifts of food from white
settlers at Fort Garry helped to sustain the first arrivals.
The contacts that they had had with whites in their homeland
stood the Santees in good stead when they arrived on Canadian
soil, and many of the men hired themselves out as farmhands,
while women secured employment as domestics in white house-
holds. Nevertheless, the Santees' early years in Canada were
times of near starvation.

Wild Plant Foods

Of the wild plant foods known in the United States, t'ípsiṇna
(Psoralea esculenta) was still to be found in Canada, although
it was not so common as in Minnesota. It is still dug and
eaten today, according to Emma Pratt and Eli Taylor (Sioux
Valley), although it is much less abundant than formerly since
fields have been plowed for farming.

Emma Pratt also mentioned "mouse beans" (Falcata comosa) as
a diet supplement. These wild beans grow in dense masses of
vines over shrubbery and other vegetation, especially along
creek banks and the edges of timber (Gilmore 1919:95). The
plant produces beans both above and below ground. The sub-
terranean beans, which are much larger than the aerial ones,
were eagerly sought by the Sioux. Field mice dig these beans

and garner them into hoards of a pint or more, and the women
would appropriate a part of these stores for their own use.
In keeping with their philosophy of maintaining an ecological
balance, the women also left some corn or other food commodity
in return for the beans that they took from the animal's
hoard.

Many other plant foods were used by the Sioux as well (see
Gilmore 1919). Various wild berries and fruits were dried and
stored for later use. Emma Pratt mentioned that the leaves of
black poplar, yatkáŋpi c'áŋ, were brewed as tea, as were rose
hips and a tall plant with narrow leaves and a blue flower
(possibly Dasystephana pubercula). Both the soft maple (Acer
saccarinum L.) and the box elder (Acer negundo L.) were tapped
for their sap, which was boiled down to make sugar. A bonus
from this sugaring activity was elm cap (Pleurotus ulmarius
Bull.), a fungus used for food, which usually grew in decayed
spots caused by tapping box elder trees for sap. Many smoking
additives are still employed by the Canadian Sioux, the most
common being sumac leaves and the inner bark of the red osier
(Cornus stolonifera), termed c'aŋšáša 'red tree' by the Sioux.
Arthur Young (Oak Lake) presented me with a generous supply of
this substance on my first visit to his home.

Hunting

Bison were still quite plentiful in the Prairie provinces when
the Santee refugees arrived, and the Santees quickly turned to
hunting them. For example, Little Crow and his followers are
reported to have joined company with a party of Red River
Métis bison hunters in 1863 (Laviolette 1944:51).

Although taking bison by the impoundment method was not a
custom of the Santees in the United States, they began to employ this technique, commonly practiced by the Plains Ojibwas,

Plains Crees, and Assiniboines, shortly after their arrival in Canada. An excellent description of this ancient hunting method was given by Charles Padani (Standing Buffalo).

A favorable locale was a broad, level plain. At one edge of this the corral or pound, a structure about fifty feet in diameter, was built of cribbed logs, with walls about twelve feet high. On the side facing the open plain a gate was prepared which could be dropped to close when the bison had been lured inside. Extending out from this gate were two log fences in a wide "V" shape. These were further extended, up to a quarter of a mile from the pound, with piles of rocks, logs, brush, and other material to form a wide funnel or chute.

When a herd of bison was noted in the vicinity of the pound a certain man, inevitably a shaman with buffalo power, known as the "buffalo caller," would disguise himself in a buffalo calf skin, complete with spike horns. Thus attired he would carefully approach the herd. By skillfully mimicking a lost calf in his actions and by bleating pitifully, the caller attempted to make the bulls that led the herd follow him. Taking a zigzag course so as not to make them suspicious, he would gradually lure them into the funnel, quickening his pace all the while. Once the herd was well into the chute, tribesmen concealed behind the stone and brush piles stood up, shouted, and waved their robes to stampede the bison at the rear of the herd. These frightened beasts would surge forward, impelling the leaders of the herd into the pound, willing or not. The buffalo caller quickly dodged to one side to save himself from being trampled to death, and made his escape. Sometimes a convenient steep bluff or gully was substituted for the pound, the bison breaking their legs as they fell over the precipice or being trampled by those behind as they crowded into the narrow gully.

Other bison hunting techniques were the surround and the
run. In the surround technique the party of hunters would
split into two files and attempt to encircle a herd and cause
it to mill. In the run, a small party of hunters would approach a herd as closely as possible, using a hill, gully, or
brush for cover, then charge in and kill as many bison as possible before the herd scattered.

The Canadian Sioux are still great hunters when the opportunity affords, and deer can be taken in the vicinity of several of the reserves. Sam Buffalo (Round Plain) said that in
hunting deer or other big game the Sioux are careful not to
run or unduly excite the quarry, as this spoils the taste of
the meat. In stalking deer, a hunter first follows the deer's
tracks for a short while to determine the general direction of
its movement. The hunter then makes a series of looping detours downwind of the deer's trail, intersecting the trail at
the end of each loop. He does this several times until he no
longer intersects the trail at the end of his loop, or until
he notices that the deer has reversed its course. This indicates that the deer has stopped to browse or bed down. The
hunter now reverses his direction and makes shorter detours,
still keeping downwind, until he surprises the deer and can
shoot it. This old Woodland hunting technique was apparently
not known to the Tetons, as Wayne Goodwill (Standing Buffalo)
recounted that he amazed his Teton relatives at Wood Mountain
by using it to take jackrabbits.

Kenneth Eastman (Oak Lake) stated that formerly Sioux hunters wore parkas with two "horns" or ear-like projections to
disguise themselves as wolves. This is no longer done, as the
hunter would be shot by trigger-happy whites in short order.
Until a few years ago Canadian Sioux hunters carried hunting
medicines with them, and sometimes the Medicine Feast was

celebrated before a major hunt to strengthen these medicines.
Mr. Eastman said that he often carried his father's medicines
when hunting and that they seemed to give him a supernatural
ability to see game.

None of my informants had ever heard of the Sioux employing
snowshoes while on the winter hunt.

The hunting of certain large birds was surrounded with
ritual and taboos. John Goodwill stated: "The old people used
to have a rule that when you killed an eagle you had to wait
four days before you plucked the feathers. They also had a
rule that when anyone killed a swan he had to make a feast
[Medicine Feast]. Old men who had medicine bags were invited.
Many times I have had a chance to kill a swan but I didn't
shoot because I didn't want to have to put up a feast like
this." Although Mr. Goodwill did not mention it, the reason
for the special treatment of the swan is probably related to
the importance of swan's-down in Santee ritual, particularly
the Medicine Dance. Swan ceremonialism is prominent in the
culture of many Woodland peoples in both the New World and the
Old.

I did not secure any accounts of the Canadian Sioux themselves practicing ritual eagle trapping of the sort known to
the Middle and Western Sioux (See Howard 1954a). Either the
practice was not known to the Santees or was abandoned some
time ago. John Goodwill, however, did recall an old Saulteaux
(Plains Ojibwa) man from Sakimay Reserve who was an expert at
trapping eagles. He would dig a pit on a bluff, cover it with
a screen of branches, and hide in it. His wife made him a
stuffed rabbit decoy which he fastened to the end of a stick
in order to manipulate it to resemble a dying rabbit. When
eagles came down to take the bait he would shoot them.

At the present time almost every young Sioux owns a .22
calibre rifle which he uses to take deer, rabbit, and porcu-

pine in the reserve area. Muskrats are still trapped for both food and pelts. Wild duck eggs are still gathered by Sioux youths and are a welcome supplement to the family diet.

Fishing

Three separate types of fishing were described to me by informants in 1972, two of which are still employed.

In 1914, while studying Canadian Sioux culture, Wallis observed a fish weir near Griswold (present Sioux Valley). He writes:

> The Wahpeton did not use fish weirs. Since moving to Manitoba, however, they have learned their construction from, they say, the Cree. The weir was constructed of branches of ash, because this wood has a rough bark that is supposed to kill fish which come into contact with it. A fish weir which the writer saw at Griswold, in the Assiniboine River, had two long converging lines which led from the banks to a trap in the middle of the stream. [1947:11]

This type of weir was described to me by Kenneth Eastman (Oak Lake), who pointed out the location of one which he had built and used for many years in the creek behind his cabin. It was essentially a brush dam with a box behind it. In the spring the fish would jump the dam and be trapped in the box.

The second type was winter ice fishing, which was described by Mr. Eastman and by Sam Buffalo (Round Plain). Mr. Buffalo employed a wire snare rather than a hook and line. First he cut a small circular hole in the river ice. Over this he would erect a small tent of poles and canvas, both to keep off the cold wind and to enable him to see the fish. He lured the

fish to the hole with a flashlight, then caught them with a
wire snare mounted on the end of a stick.

Those Sioux living near the larger lakes in Saskatchewan,
such as on the Standing Buffalo Reserve, engaged in commercial
fishing with boats and long nets. John Goodwill commented:

> I used to be a great fisherman. I had a one
> hundred foot net and we would sweep the lake [Fish-
> ing Lakes] with it once east and west and once
> north and south. Sometimes we would get several
> hundred pounds of fish. I would sell most of these
> in town. You can still get fish in this lake, but
> since the lake turned green, they aren't fit to
> eat.

Animal Husbandry

Even before their flight to Canada, the Santees owned extensive herds of horses. Unfortunately, we lack accurate information as to how many, or how many were lost in the difficult
early years. Certainly, to older Santees, the horse looms
only slightly less important than to the Tetons and other High
Plains tribes.

Kenneth Eastman said that the common way employed by the
Santees to break a wild horse was first to lasso it. Then two
mounted men would ride up on it, one on either side. From one
of these a third man, who had been riding double, would mount
the wild horse. The horse would be able to buck, but not to
spin or roll on the ground. Pete Lethbridge (Wood Mountain)
described a different technique employed by the Tetons of his
reserve. An old man named Good Track, he said, would break
horses by riding them in water or deep snow. He himself
breaks horses by tying up one of the hind feet so that the

animal has only three legs and can't kick. He gradually accustoms the horse to the blanket by throwing it on his back and then removing it, repeating this several times. He does the same with the saddle. When the horse is used to this he mounts and dismounts several times. After the horse becomes accustomed to the weight of a man on his back, a snaffle bit is put on and the horse is taught to respond to the reins. In this manner the horse is tamed but its spirit is not broken. Sometimes, Mr. Lethbridge says, he must "ear down" a horse, that is, grab the horse's ears and bite them, which is so painful that the animal will stand still. Formerly, he said, before there were bucking chutes, horses were "eared down" at rodeos.

Some information on Sioux horse lore was provided by Charles Padani (Standing Buffalo). The Santees, he said, doctored their horses by blowing herb medicines into the animals' nostrils. They also "cracked the veins" of horses (bled them) when they were ill, just as they did with human patients. To prepare a horse for use in battle the animal's tail was tied up in red cloth and wasé wak'áŋ, protective red paint, was used to decorate it. The bullets of the enemy, according to Mr. Padani, would simply glance off horses so protected. He also reported the Sioux belief that if you kill a magpie and tie it around the neck of a mare coming to foal, it will ensure that the colt will be a pinto.

According to Mr. Padani, the Santees raised various kinds of dogs for different purposes. A particularly large type was kept to pull the travois. One type, still present on several Sioux reserves, is called istá tópa 'four eyes' because it has two tan spots on the otherwise black hair of its head.

The Sioux did not have a special class of names used only for dogs. Instead, human names were used, such as C'aské

'First-born Son', Hoksína 'Boy', and Wic'íŋcana 'Girl'. Occasionally wild coyote or fox pups were raised as pets.

Mr. Padani also reported that the Sioux considered magpies,
uŋkcék'iña 'defecates laughing', to be easily tamed as pets.

Horticulture and Food Preservation

Gardening languished among the Sioux in the years immediately
following their arrival in Canada, but after settling on reserves the women once again began to plant small gardens of
corn, pumpkins, and beans. According to Emma Pratt, these
three crops, the "three sisters" of Woodland Indians, were
interplanted. Sometimes the pumpkin vines were allowed to
climb the trunks of elm trees growing near the garden patch.
Mrs. Pratt recalled the harvest season as a pleasant, busy
time. When all the crops were in the men and boys would busy
themselves preparing the houses for winter while the women
dried corn for winter use.

Farming and cattle raising had been adopted by some Santee
men even before the flight to Canada, and once settled on reserves, more of them took up the husbandman's crafts. As early as 1877 a delegation of Santee chiefs, including Standing
Buffalo and White Cap, petitioned Lieutenant Governor Laird at
Fort Pelly for a reserve, agricultural implements, and seed
grains. Laird declined to give them a reserve but offered to
try to obtain seed and agricultural implements for them (Laviolette 1944:16-17). By 1900 there were many prosperous
Canadian Santee farmers, and farming continued to be the most
important source of income on most reserves until after World
War II. Several older male informants in 1972 spoke proudly
of their farming operations and produced snapshots of themselves with teams and farming machinery. After the war, however, the increased mechanization of farming and the capital

investment in farm machinery required by this forced many families out of farming and into wage labor. This phenomenon, by
no means limited to American Indian farmers, particularly mil-
itated against Indians because they lacked a tradition of ac-
cumulating capital to invest in machinery or to add to their
land base. Today only a few men on each reserve are full-time
farmers. On the Standing Buffalo Reserve, for example, where
forty years ago almost all of the adult males operated farms
or were employed as farmhands, only four were so engaged in
1972.

Cattle raising, often combined with farming, has been an
important source of income at White Cap, Wood Mountain, and
Sioux Valley. At Wood Mountain and White Cap I was told that
the Sioux communities were almost completely self-supporting,
although at the latter the cattle raising operation had been
crippled by government confiscation of a large part of the
range land for use by the adjacent military camp.

Until a few years ago, meat was preserved for future use by
drying. It was cut in thin slices (following the musculature,
not cutting across it), and dried on scaffolds high enough to
be out of reach of camp dogs and wild scavengers. It might be
smoked to speed the drying process, after which it was packed
into rawhide parfleches or canvas bags. Some meat was pounded
up and mixed with tallow and pounded chokecherries or buffalo
berries to make pemican. Today freezers are employed by most
Sioux families to preserve their meat, but a few still make
jerky in the old manner. At a powwow in 1972 I observed
strips of fresh meat drying on the luggage rack of an automo-
bile.

Housing and Settlement

Apparently the Santees gave up building their gable-roofed

bark summer lodges when they left Minnesota. The wak'éya or
tent (the structures termed "tipis" by whites) and the t'i-
úktaŋ or domed lodge (called "wickiups" by whites) became the
year round dwellings for the Santees during their first years
on Canadian soil.

The first log cabins were built in the late 1870s on the
Birdtail Reserve, a fact memorialized in the present name for
this reserve, C'aŋkáǧa Ot'í 'Dwellers In Log Cabins'. From
here their use spread to all the Canadian reserves. Some log
cabins are still in use today, but are rapidly being replaced
by small frame buildings erected by Sioux men with the aid of
government grants.

These frame dwellings are the most salient features in a
reserve community. They are small by the standards of Canadian culture at large, but are cheerfully painted, inside and
out, and for the most part are kept clean and tidy. Scattered
on the hills and valleys of the reserve, and connected to one
another by beeline footpaths, they present a distinctively
American Indian settlement pattern. Some householders decorate the outside of their dwelling with bright geometric designs such as the Uŋktómi t'ahókmu 'Spider's web', and have
neat flower beds flanking the doorway. A steepled church or
two, a school, sports field, and the tribal office building
complete the picture.

Formerly most Sioux reserves also boasted an octagonal
dance hall, a log or frame building derived from the earth-
lodge of the Missouri River tribes. These structures, used
for winter performances of the Grass Dance and associated
social dances, have now disappeared but are fondly remembered.
Exactly why they have not been replaced no one can say. Certainly there is an expressed need for such a public hall on
many reserves.

Several of my older informants boasted that they had been born and spent their early years in a canvas tipi. Pleasant enough in summer, a tipi may leave something to be desired in winter. Sam Buffalo (Round Plain) mentioned that he and some friends tried to "tough it out" all winter in a tent, but were driven indoors when the mercury dipped to forty degrees below zero. To make the tipi habitable in winter, a canvas liner some four feet high and long enough to circle the tipi was fastened to the poles inside. Evergreen or willow boughs were piled thickly on the floor of the lodge except in the center, where the fire blazed.

Today the tipi serves mainly as a reminder of the old way for the Canadian Sioux. At powwows and fairs the sponsors will endeavor to secure as many tipis as possible and have them erected near the "big top" or dancing arena. This provides an appropriately "Indian" atmosphere, and the tipis can be used to house guests who have not brought their own tents. Chief William Eagle of White Cap has no fewer than six tipis that he transports to various powwows and sets up. At Sioux Valley I noticed a small but nicely set up and decorated tipi beside a regular frame dwelling. I was told that the owner had set it up as an exhibit.

In the old days, when on the move, the Canadian Sioux employed both the hupák'iŋ or travois and the Red River cart. Small children, the very aged, and the ill would ride on the travois or in the cart bed, which was also used to transport the lodge cover and parfleches containing the household food and equipment. Tipi poles were either put in bunches on both sides of a horse (a different one from that pulling the travois) or lashed to the sides of the cart, the thinner ends projecting out behind.

Technology and Crafts

Most of the technology employed in the daily existence of
Canadian Sioux at the present is that of the non-Indian world.
The pickup truck, hay rake, post hole auger, carpenter tools,
are all from the white man's culture. Only where there is
no adequate European-derived substitute do aboriginal tech-
nological skills continue, mostly in the area of arts and
crafts.

At Sioux Valley one old lady still makes fine, serviceable
baskets of willow twigs. They are made of two colors, using
peeled and unpeeled twigs, and strongly resemble a common O-
jibwa and Plains Ojibwa style. I was informed that this lady
works at her basketry only during the winter and that her entire output is contracted for ahead of time by collectors in
eastern Canada.

Charles Padani (Standing Buffalo) was the only informant to
mention pottery making as a Santee craft. His account indicated a basic knowledge of ceramics, although he said he had
never actually seen pots made. He said that a type of white
stone (probably "rotten granite") was heated, then crumbled
and used to temper the clay. Pots were hand modeled, dried,
then fired. No pottery has been produced by the Canadian
Sioux for at least two generations.

Mr. Padani also described the technique of stone boiling
cookery, and said that his great grandfather had employed it.
The hide of a bison's head was used as the container. It was
set up on four stakes and filled with water and the pieces of
meat which were to be cooked. Four stones were heated in a
fire nearby. As each became red hot it was lifted with tongs
and dropped into the soup. When it had cooled it was replaced
by another stone, and the process repeated until the soup had
boiled long enough to cook the meat.

Flint knapping is a technique so long forgotten by the
Sioux that the occasional flint projectile points which they
find are termed Uŋktómi kâǧapi 'produced by Spider', the
Trickster-culture hero, and are not considered to be man made.

Some Sioux can still make serviceable bows and arrows, although they are no longer used for hunting and are mainly
children's toys. I examined an excellent bow made by George
High Eagle (Oak Lake). It was made of ash and was of the self
type, double-curved, rectangular in cross section, and about
four feet long.

Chief William Eagle (White Cap) produces excellent hand
drums of the single-head, tambour type. The frame is made by
steaming and bending a thin, flat piece of wood into a circle.
Holes are drilled into each end and the ends are sewed together with sinew. A wet piece of hide is laced over the frame so
that it covers one face of the drum and the sides. It is
tightened by means of a drawstring inserted through several
cuts made in the outer margin of the drumhead. Twisted rawhide thongs are crossed on the underside to provide a hand
grip. Once the wet hide has dried, it is tight enough to produce a booming tone. Chief Eagle also makes fine traditional-
style pipestems. I saw a few Indian pipes of the prow type,
made both of catlinite and what is called "blackstone" (shale
rubbed with grease and soot). Some of these, all older speci-
mens, were inlaid with pewter or lead. Several of my older
male informants, learning that I was from the United States,
inquired if it would be possible to secure catlinite, the red
pipestone, from the famous quarries near Pipestone, Minnesota.
On my return trip to Oklahoma I secured a supply of the pre-
cious material from Minnesota Santees who work at the quarries
and mailed it to Canada.

Beadwork and Quillwork

The Canadian Sioux still produce large amounts of fine beadwork in both floral and geometric designs. Almost all of this
is used in dancing costumes. The spot or overlay stitch
(sewn directly to the hide or cloth) and loomwork are the most
common techniques. Lazy stitch appears occasionally on moccasins, and wrapped beadwork is used on such items as purse
handles and the loop elements in "Crow" necklaces and girls'
braid ties.

I saw a few magnificent matching floral beadwork costumes
(including Archie Eagle's of White Cap, Gordon Taylor's of
Sioux Valley, and Daniel Sutherland's of Oak Lake), but matching geometric design costumes were more common. More common
still were mixtures of floral and geometric designs in a single costume. Floral design beadwork, although it has been
produced by the Santees for at least a century, is still
termed "Chippewa" or "Cree" work by Sioux beadworkers. At
Wood Mountain I was told that only "long flowers" (bilaterally
symmetrical floral work in lazy stitch technique, the floral
elements being very narrow and elongated) were characteristically Sioux. Even on this largely Teton reserve, however, Mrs.
Pete Lethbridge makes beautiful realistic floral beadwork.
Floral beadwork does seem to be slightly more common at Sioux
Valley and Oak Lake, although it is still being produced at
all eight Canadian Sioux reserves.

Porcupine quillwork is also still produced, although it is
much less common than beadwork. Two women at Standing Buffalo
are said to produce porcupine quillwork, one at Round Plain,
and one at Wood Mountain, but I did not see any examples of
their work. What little quillwork is produced is ordered in
advance by dancers for their costumes. We saw none for sale.

Craft cooperatives, largely devoted to retailing beadwork and leatherwork, have been established at Sioux Valley and Standing Buffalo. Unfortunately, the demands of the commercial market have led to a debasement of native craft techniques at both places. Thus at Sioux Valley the moccasins produced are of commercially tanned leather rather than buckskin, are of a non-Sioux style, and are characterized by an ugly ridge of leather (sewed with a sewing machine) in place of the delicate puckering and silk-wrapped horsehair edging that surrounds the vamp of traditional moccasins of this type.

Today it is common to see black beads in Canadian Sioux beadwork, but they were not used before about 1930, because black was considered the color of death. Wayne Goodwill (Standing Buffalo) had heard older people say that every item of beadwork should have an odd bead, that is, a bead that is obviously of the wrong color or out of place in the design. This custom is also reported for the Sioux at Fort Totten by Edward Milligan and Louis Garcia (personal communications). The reason is said to be that only Wakan Tanka (God) is perfect, and therefore it is presumptuous for man to attempt perfection in a craft item. However, Mrs. Steve Goodwill had never neard of this tradition. Nor had she or her husband ever heard that beadwork designs could be family property among the Sioux. This custom is reported by Mr. and Mrs. Louis Garcia at Fort Totten, who showed me a design belonging to the Red Fox family, of which Mrs. Garcia is a member.

Although buckskin is still highly valued by the Sioux as the base for beaded women's dresses, men's shirts and leggings, and other large items, present day beadworkers sometimes substitute heavy canvas as the backing for solid-beaded pieces. Mrs. Alex Goodwill (Standing Buffalo) showed us a beaded yoke done on canvas backing being made by her daughter to ornament a buckskin dress.

Clothing

For all occasions except ceremonial dances the garb of the Canadian Sioux is the same as that of other Canadians. Only occasionally does one now see an older man or woman wearing
buckskin moccasins, the last item of aboriginal dress to be
replaced by a commercial substitute. Heirloom photographs
from the 1880s and 1890s show women wearing cloth costumes
somewhat similar to the aboriginal buckskin dress, either with
blouse and skirt separate or cut from the same piece. Moccasins, numerous bead necklaces, and a shawl completed the costume. Men often appear wearing a choker necklace with a circular shell (kaŋpéska) at the front, a European style shirt,
vest, and frock coat, plus a breechcloth and leggings of
stroud cloth, beaded kneebands with yarn ties, and moccasins.
Martha Tawiyaka (Standing Buffalo) recalled men wearing white
cotton shirts cut like the older buckskin garments. Often
these had painted designs indicating horses stolen (hoofprints) or enemies killed (crosses). The fringes were painted
with vermillion (wasé). She also remembered men wearing kneebands of skunk, fox, or badger hide. Skunk hide kneebands,
the sign of a successful warrior, were also remembered by Jim
Kiyewakan (Sioux Valley). He mentioned one old man of his reserve who boasted that as a youth he had worn skunk skin kneebands, armbands, and even a turban of twisted skunk skin. "I
really dressed well when I wore those," he is quoted as saying.

George Bear (Birdtail) remembered that old time Sioux men
prized otter skins, both for turbans and for the ptaŋhá
wanáp'iŋ, a necklace of tanned otter skin decorated with rows
of small round trade mirrors. Wayne Goodwill (Standing Buffalo) spoke of his plans to make one of these for his dancing
costume.

Sam Buffalo (Round Plain) mentioned that the Hudson's Bay Company yarn sash (itself a loomed imitation of the finger-woven Indian originals) was widely used as a turban (ité siŋdá), a belt (icáske ip'íyake 'belt that ties together'), and a shoulder sash or baldric (wac'útik'iŋ 'something laying across the body'). He also mentioned that when an old-time Sioux youth wore a skunk tail sewed at the heel of his moccasin this indicated that he was looking for a wife.

The Canadian Sioux share their most common moccasin styles with both the Plains Ojibwas and the Plains Crees. Both styles are soft soled. The first has a small vamp, usually solidly beaded, and a short seam that extends from the vamp to the front of the moccasin top. The leather of the remainder of the moccasin is puckered around this tongue and seam to shape the moccasin to the foot. The tongue usually has an edging of silk or moosehair wrapped around several strands of horsehair. This moccasin style has a beaded cuff that matches the design of the tongue. Only overlay or spot stitch bead-work is used on this type of moccasin, which clearly reflects the Woodland background of the Santees.

The second type seems to be a copy of the Plains hard sole style, but has a soft sole. Often the entire upper part of this type of moccasin is beaded. This type seems to be more popular on the Saskatchewan reserves. It is the dominant style at Wood Mountain, and even there the technique of making hard soled moccasins seems to have been lost. This type of moccasin is often decorated with lazy-stitch beadwork, and probably reflects a Plains Indian borrowing by those Santees who now use it. Several of my informants were amazed when I showed them a pair of hard soled moccasins from the United States, and could not figure out how moccasins with such in-flexible soles could be turned inside out during the manufacturing process when the uppers were sewn to the soles.

The roach headdress is the most prized item of costuming
among the Canadian Sioux today (cf. Howard 1960b). Living in
an area where the long haired Canadian porcupine is abundant,
the Sioux, together with the neighboring Plains Crees, Assiniboines, and Plains Ojibwas, have the finest headdresses of
this type anywhere in the Plains. All four of these tribes
trade, sell, and give away fine roaches to dancers from the
United States, some of whom travel hundreds of miles to visit
well known roach makers.

The best roaches are those with a completely hair base,
that is, a center foundation composed entirely of clipped
fringes of deerhair sewed together. Hair base roaches are now
becoming rare, however, and today braided yarn or strips cut
from an old felt hat are often substituted for the base material. Such roaches are frowned upon and termed "imitations"
by older Sioux. At the outer edge of this base, however constituted, two rows of unclipped deer hair fringe are sewn,
then two fringes of porcupine hair, and finally one or two
more fringes of deer hair, either dyed a bright red or left
natural white. A hole in the center of the base toward the
front serves to fasten the roach to the wearer's head, either
by means of a beaded harness or a shoestring tied under the
chin. A similar thong at the back ties the tail of the headdress around the wearer's neck.

Wayne Goodwill, one of the leading dancers at Standing Buffalo, said that a roach headdress should be combed periodically and the hair oiled to prevent its becoming dry. He uses
Brylcreem hair oil on his. He also washes his headdress every
so often to keep the white deer hair clean. To keep a roach
headdress in its correct shape when not in use, and to prevent
the hair from breaking, it is stored on a stick and wrapped
entirely around with an elastic bandage.

Arthur Young and his wife (Oak Lake) make roach headdresses as a regular supplementary source of income, pur-
chasing deer and porcupine hair from local youths. They use
a bow loom on which to tie the component fringes of deer and
porcupine hair. The loom has two warp threads. These are al-
ternately separated by punching an empty wooden thread spool
and threading it on one of the warp threads. The fringe is
produced by half hitching small bunches of animal hair around
the warp threads. Some roach makers dispense with the bow
loom, simply tying the warp threads to a nail in the wall at
one end and to their belt at the other. A finished Canadian
Sioux roach headdress has a low profile in comparison with
those of the Central and Southern Plains, and is much longer
in the tail. In 1972 a finished roach headdress sold for $50
to $70, thus providing a substantial increment to the income
of the maker. One dancer from Sioux Village wore a roach
headdress made of plastic fiber in place of the traditional
porcupine hair.

Children

The Sioux infant was ushered into the world with the assistance of a midwife, generally a female relative of the mother.
This woman cut and tied the umbilical cord and wiped the baby
dry. Should the mother experience difficulty in bearing the
child, the midwife might administer an herb decoction to the
mother. George Bear (Birdtail) said that his father possessed
such a "midwife herb." This plant was dried, ground up, and
mixed with rattlesnake fat. It made the unborn child afraid,
causing it to come out of the mother's womb. Scaring the baby
out of the womb was also the theory behind a Heyoka (anti-
natural clown) being called in to assist in a difficult birth
on the Standing Buffalo Reserve in an incident mentioned by
John Goodwill. The place of birth, for most of my older informants, was the family tipi. Several mentioned that they
had been "born in a tipi," a boast akin to the nineteenth century politician's claim to having been born in a log cabin.

John Goodwill (Standing Buffalo) stated that the first-born
son in a family was put in a highly decorated wap'óstaŋ (baby
cradle hood), often completely decorated with quillwork or
beadwork. Since it had taken months to manufacture and would
be used only a short time, this wapóstan was designed so that
the beaded or quilled pieces on either side could later be
used as shoulder ornaments on the boy's dancing costume.
John's own wapóstan was used in this way when he was sixteen
years old. The Plains Ojibwas also practiced a similar
custom.

The baby's umbilical cord was dried and preserved in a
small buckskin pouch, which was regarded as an amulet or

talisman. John Goodwill commented that he still has his umbilical cord pouch and that it brings him luck.

The Sioux cradle was either of the wapostan type, to the
back of which wooden supports could be attached for rigidity,
or was a solid wooden board to which a bent wooden bow was
attached at the top, and a cloth bag to hold the baby attached
further down. In both types the infant was placed in the
pouch, which was laced up and bound around with buckskin
thongs so that only the baby's head appeared. Before lacing
up the bag, moss was placed between the infant's legs to ab-
sorb excrement. The cradle could then be carried in the mother's arms, on her back by means of a strap, or could be slung
from the saddle horn when the mother was riding. When she was
working in her garden or tanning hides, the cradle could be
set up nearby or hung on a tree limb.

Since the infant could not move his arms and legs in such a
cradle, the child was removed from time to time to be bathed
and to exercise. When the mother was working in the tipi or
house, the baby was often placed in a baby hammock. This hammock, generally slung in a corner of a room or between two
poles in a tipi, would be pushed gently from time to time to
rock the baby. Such hammocks went out of use only recently
according to Sam Buffalo (Round Plain).

When he was still quite small, the child's paternal grandfather pierced his ears for earrings. This was a ceremonial
act and was accompanied by a distribution of gifts by the parents. It served to introduce the child, as a distinct person-
ality, to the members of the tribe. Kenneth Eastman (Oak
Lake) recalled his own ear piercing and also that his grandfather had given him a necklace of muskrat paws when he was
very small. He commented, "A muskrat is a hard worker, and
this was supposed to make me a hard worker, too."

Sioux children learned by observing adults and were incorporated into adult activities as soon as their coordination
and strength permitted. Games like cup and pin and hoop and
pole also taught coordination. Legends told around the camp-
fire in winter provided object lessons in human behavior. The
folktales involving Uŋktómi (Spider), the mischievous anti-
hero of the Sioux, were particularly valuable in this respect,
teaching in a humorous manner the folly of excessive vanity,
envy, boastfulness, and other human frailties. These stories
are still favorites today. Other stories exemplified for
Sioux children the wonders of the natural world and man's
weakness when confronted with the spiritual beings that
governed it. Stories of great warriors of the past and tales
of sisterly devotion provided models for expected adult behavior.

Courtship and Marriage

Dakota girls married at about age eighteen, while boys generally took a wife at age twenty. Romantic love was certainly a
factor, but a man's qualities as a hunter and warrior, a woman's as a tanner of hides and seamstress, probably weighed
heavier. Courting involved flirting at public ceremonies and
formal courtship in the evening and early part of the night.
One form of courtship involved a youth serenading his heart's
desire using the c'ót'aŋka or courting flute (see Deloria and
Brandon, 1961). These flutes, although superficially similar
to the śiyót'aŋka or Grass Dance whistles, are actually quite
different. The courting flute is larger in diameter and is
equipped with five stops or finger holes. The flute was blown
from the upper end. The lower end was sometimes carved to
resemble a garfish head. These flutes were generally made of
cedar wood. After being roughed out, the billet was carefully

split, hollowed, and the two sections glued together with fish
or hoof glue. To make the flute airtight at the seams, the
pericardium (heart skin) of a bison was sometimes stretched
over the tube. The flute was tuned by adjusting a carved
wooden block, termed the "saddle," over the sound hole at the
upper end. Once a flute was tuned this saddle was glued in
place. Jim Kiyewakan (Sioux Valley) recalled once seeing a
particularly fine flute that had a saddle made of the sacred
red pipestone, and I once saw an entire flute made of this
material. Both Jim Kiyewakan and Archie Eagle (White Cap)
recalled fondly the sound of these courting flutes throughout
the countryside on a summer evening. They are a facet of
Sioux culture now completely vanished.

A youth, having flirted with a girl at a dance, and perhaps
having received some sign of encouragement from her, would
position himself on a hill near her parental home and sing or
play love songs on his flute. The girl, if she were interested, would attempt to go out to meet him, perhaps on the pre-
text of getting a pail of water or gathering an armload of
wood. Since Dakota girls were closely chaperoned by mothers
and aunts, there was usually only time for the exchange of a
few words, the couple wrapped in the boy's blanket or robe.

A few old love songs were recalled by Sioux informants in
Canada, who allowed me to tape them. The following two were
sung by Robert Good Voice (Round Plain).

> Úŋšiya iš táku káyake.
> T'awícu yat'úŋke.
> Táku sáŋpa yac'íŋ he?
>
> Have some pity.
> You are married.
> What more do you want?

Dé yuhá miyéksuya ye. (four times)
Itéowapi kiŋ dé yaúŋ kte.

Keeping this, remember me!
With this photograph you will live.

Archie Eagle (White Cap) sang the following love song.

Ektá mayá ináhma sic'é,
Ináhma waŋmáyaŋka.
Iyóhpemayiŋ kta.

Secretly he starts toward me, my brother-in-law,
Secretly he sees me.
He will throw me away.

The Canadian Sioux still recall marriage by purchase.
Frank Merrick (Long Plain) said that marriage was always by
purchase in the old days. He commented:

A horse was given to the parents of the bride.
If they accepted it and the girl was willing, the
marriage was announced. The new bride and groom,
though, slept apart for four nights before having
intercourse. This is a good custom. The boy and
girl are both very nervous at this time, and are
still not used to one another. Many marriages
are spoiled nowadays by the bride and groom having
intercourse before they are at ease with one another.

Emma Pratt (Sioux Valley) recalled: "Some men paid horses for
their bride. I was paid for in this way myself. I guess I
wasn't such a good prospect, since my husband only gave three
horses for me."

Kin Groups

Writing of Minnesota Santee social organization during the first half of the nineteenth century, Landes notes: "Members of each Santee village considered themselves actual close kin, who generally married out of the kin circle and natal village. Behavior within the village was always determined by kin prescriptions" (1968:95). By and large this statement is still true for the Canadian Sioux of the present day. On some of the smaller reserves, such as White Cap and Wood Mountain, almost every individual is genetically related to everyone else, and young people must look outside the reserve for marriage partners. Recently there have been numerous marriages of Sioux men to Plains Cree, Plains Ojibwa, and Assiniboine girls as a direct result of this.

On the larger reserves, such as Standing Buffalo and Sioux Valley, one finds a number of separate patrilineages, among which strong love-hate relationships pertain. Backbiting gossip and even character assassination of one patrilineage by members of another is common, but these same groups quickly close ranks when challenged by outsiders from another tribe or the white man's world. Thus at the 1972 Standing Buffalo powwow, an older man paraded about the powwow grounds loudly singing an honor song in praise of Chief Standing Buffalo, and by implication, the patrilineage stemming from this chief, of which he was a member. After his song he loudly and bitterly remarked, in both Dakota and English, that the Standing Buffalo patrilineage was the chiefly lineage on this reserve, not the Goodwill lineage, which was the group responsible for that year's powwow. The same man, however, was later heard boasting about how much better the powwows on his reserve were than those at Sinta Luta, a nearby Assiniboine reserve.

Lineage ties are quite evident in church membership, where all the members of a patrilineage, together with their spouses, are liable to belong to the same sect. Thus at Standing Buffalo it is largely the Goodfeather lineage that supports the newly introduced Evangelical church, having deserted the Roman Catholic faith en masse to do so. At Sioux Village the Smoke patrilineage turned Evangelical in 1970. At the latter reserve it was this patrilineage that had been most active in promoting Indian dances and other Indian activities, and this sudden conversion dealt a death blow to the customary summer powwow there.

Members of a patrilineage support one another economically, assist one another in ceremonial obligations such as the customary giveaway at the summer powwow, and constantly visit one another for days or weeks at a time. Capital goods are generally vested in the older men. Thus, at Sioux Valley, I noticed several farm trucks with the proud inscription painted on the side, "_____ and sons, Sioux Valley, Manitoba." At the present time, when off reservation employment and residence is increasing, the home of that son who has established himself in Winnipeg, Brandon, Regina, or Saskatoon will serve as the temporary home for brothers, nephews, and nieces seeking employment or attending school in the city.

Kinship System

At all eight Canadian Sioux reserves the traditional Dakota (bifurcate merging) kinship system is still employed. It shows no sign of breakdown or of progression to another type. This type of kinship system, sometimes termed the Dakota-Iroquois type, distinguishes sharply between a parental sibling of the same sex as the parent on that side of the family and one of the opposite sex. It likewise distinguishes a cross

cousin (mother's brother's or father's sister's child) from a
parallel cousin (mother's sister's or father's brother's
child). Parallel cousins are equated with Ego's genetic sib-
lings, and their parents are "mother" and "father" to Ego,
whereas cross cousins are addressed by "cousin" terms and
their parents are "uncles" and "aunts."

It is important to note, however, that the Sioux refer to
the children of cross cousins of the opposite sex as "nephew"
and "niece," not as "son" and "daughter" as is the case among
the neighboring Ojibwas. This probably indicates that cross-
cousin marriage, often associated with the bifurcate merging
type kinship system, has not been practiced by the Sioux for
a considerable length of time (cf. Dole 1972:150-154). Where
cross-cousin marriage is the norm, one would call the children
of one's cross cousin of the opposite sex "son" and "daughter"
as this cross cousin would be the preferred mate. Where this
is not the case, as with the Sioux, one imagines that the importance of maintaining regular and stable intergroup alli-
ances through cross-cousin marriage has ceased to be important. That cross-cousin marraige was once practiced by the
Sioux is indicated by the fact that the cross cousin relationship "allowed participants extensive and boorish flirting
privileges" (Landes 1968:98), probably a relic of earlier
times. However, both Landes' 1935 Minnesota Santee informants
and my 1972 Canadian Sioux informants were universal in condemning cross-cousin marriage as incestuous.

Although they lacked the strong clan system and cross generation (Omaha or Crow) kinship system of such groups as the
Kickapoos, Potawatomis, Winnebagos, Iowas, Omahas, Poncas,
Mandans, and Hidatsas, in their total cultural configuration
the Santees were quite similar to these groups. At the same
time the Santees and Ojibwas did share an enormous number of

specific culture traits and complexes. Items of costume, ar-
tistic traditions, weapons for war and the chase, and above
all, the Medicine Lodge organization (the Ojibwa Midewiwin,
the Santee Wakan Wacipi), bear witness to this long cultural
interchange. The curious absence of clans among the Santees,
in which they differ from all of the surrounding tribes, poses
a problem. Why do the Santees stand alone among all the
groups in the Upper Midwest in their lack of named, corporate,
exogamic kinship groups? Landes suggests that the Santee village, which possessed many of the characteristics of the clans
of the Central Algonquians and Southern Siouans, obviated the
need for such groupings (1968:28, 29, 79 footnote 11; cf.
Howard 1979).

Wallis noted in 1914 the classificatory levirate and s19ror-
ate among the Canadian Santees (1947:31). It is no longer
practiced at the present time but was remembered by my informants, as was sororal polygyny.

Ordinal terms for children have largely fallen into disuse.
Martha Tawiyaka and John Goodwill (both of Standing Buffalo)
remembered the following:

First born son	C'aské	First born daughter	Winóna
Second born son	Hepáŋ	Second born daughter	Hápaŋ
Third born son	Hepí		

Neither informant recalled the remaining terms in the series:
C'atáŋ and Haké for the fourth and fifth sons in a family, and
Hápistiŋna, Wáŋske, and Wiháke for the third, fourth, and
fifth born daughters (Riggs 1893:45).

The parents of a bridal pair considered themselves to be
related, and called one another omáwahet'uŋ.

Visiting

Visiting, particularly visiting relatives at other reserves,
could probably be termed the favorite entertainment of the
Canadian Sioux. Attendance at the large summer powwows is
probably as much for visiting as for actual participation in
the singing and dancing. If a family has no actual kinfolk at
a certain reserve, often a fictive kinship bond will be established between the heads of two patrilineages, and the family
members will exchange visits at their reserve's powwows. On
the occasion of such visits it is common for the host family
to bestow handsome gifts upon their guests, either informally
or at an itúh'aṇpi or formal giveaway held in connection with
each powwow. The first visit of a stranger to a Sioux home is
also marked by a handsome gift if the family is at all able to
do so.

John Goodwill (Standing Buffalo) recounted an anecdote that
exemplifies Sioux generosity:

> When I was younger I was a great dancer and my
> womenfolk made me a beautiful dancing costume with
> lots of beadwork and quillwork. Some parts of
> this costume were from my wapoštan [hood for baby
> cradle]. Well, we had a big dance here on Novem-
> ber 11, Armistice Day, and my cousin and his folks
> came up here from Poplar [Montana] for a visit.
> I was dressing for the dance and my cousin admired
> my costume. I said to him, "I am going to give
> you these clothes to take home with you right
> after the dance tonight." So I gave up my beauti-
> ful costume. A couple of years later I visited
> him at his place in Montana and he and his folks
> gave me a new dancing costume, but it didn't com-
> pare with the one I had given him.

Athletic Sports

At the present time baseball or softball is the chief summer
sport of the Canadian Sioux, and (where facilities permit) ice
hockey is the favorite winter sport among younger men, just as
it is among non-Indian Canadians. At Sioux Valley I was
proudly directed to the newly established sports field where
baseball, horseshoes, and various track and field events are
held each summer on "Sports Day" and other less formal occasions. The tribal council at Sioux Valley has been trying for
a number of years to secure funds from the government for a
hockey rink.

The older traditional games of the Sioux, such as lacrosse,
shinny, and various archery games, have not been played for
years and in fact are scarcely remembered. Of the various
traditional field games only hoop and pole was recalled by my
informants. Sam Buffalo said that hoop and pole had been
played at Round Plain and George Bear (age 93) had seen it
played at Birdtail when he was a youth. Wooden hoops, varying
in size from a foot to less than three inches in diameter,
filled with rawhide netting, were employed in this game.
These were rolled across a level piece of ground and two men
trotted after, hurling spear-like poles at the hoop in an attempt to pierce the netting and stop it. The player worked
from the largest hoop down to the smallest.

Sam Buffalo also remembered the game of tops, c'aŋká
wac'îpi 'wood they cause to dance'. The tops were made from
the tips of bison horns, with a plume (for balance) inserted
in the hollow upper end. The top was lashed with a rawhide
whip to make it spin and players vied with one another to see
who could make his top spin the longest. Sam commented that
he had kept a top for many years that had belonged to his
father.

Gambling Games

The moccasin game, which is termed hą́pa ap'éda ('to strike
moccasins') in the Eastern dialect and hą́pa mahéyuzapi ('to
mix up inside moccasins') in the Middle dialect, is still
played by the Canadian Sioux, although it is not as common as
it was a decade ago. Until recently it was customary to have
at least one session of moccasin game at each summer powwow,
and I recall witnessing in the 1950s several games at Fort
Totten, North Dakota, which pitted the local Sioux against
their Canadian visitors. It was also customary, in North
Dakota and Canada, to play for about a week during the month
of January. Heavy betting, often of items of clothing, usually accompanies the games.

Rules of the game were secured from John Goodwill (Standing
Buffalo) and Kenneth Eastman (Oak Lake), both acknowledged ex-
perts. Four pads (originally actual moccasins) are used, and
the person selected by the team as the hider places a large
bead under one of the four. The guesser, selected from the
opposing team, has a long stick with which to strike or turn
the moccasins. Twenty wooden sticks, about the size of lead
pencils, are used as counters.

The object of the game is to strike on the first guess the
moccasin under which the hider has placed the bead. The hider
has done this with much feinting, bobbing his head and body in
time to the moccasin game songs and drumming which are an in-
tegral part of the game. If the guesser misses the correct
moccasin the first time, on his second guess he must endeavor
to "push a blank," that is, guess a moccasin which does not
hide the bead. If the guesser hits the moccasin that conceals
the bead the first time he wins four sticks from the pile of
counters that has been placed between the two groups of con-
testants at the start of the game. He also wins the right for

his side to hide next. If the guesser misses the bead on his
first guess but succeeds in "pushing a blank" on his second
guess, the guesser's side loses two sticks. If he misses on
the first time and is also unfortunate enough to hit the moccasin hiding the bead on his second guess, his side loses four
sticks. The game goes on in this way until one side has won
all of the sticks from the middle as well as all those won
from the middle by their opponents. Each side replaces its
hider and its guesser from time to time, usually when these
individuals have had a string of bad luck.

When the guesser's side has only four sticks remaining and
all of the sticks have been won from the middle, the hider may
take away two of the moccasins from the four in front of him
and say, "ohu." This is a challenge to the guesser. If the
guesser misses the bead the hiders have won the game. If the
guesser hits the bead with these favorable odds, he wins four
sticks and the game goes on.

Another end game maneuver is the ak'énuŋpa or "twelve"
play. In this case all of the pads are left in place. The
striker's side has only two counting sticks remaining, having
missed on the previous play and "pushed a blank" on the second
guess. The hider's side holds six sticks, and the other
twelve are placed in the middle. If the striker hits the bead
the first time he gets the twelve sticks. If he misses, the
twelve sticks stay in the middle. If he strikes a blank on
the first guess but succeeds in hitting the bead on the second, the hiders get eight sticks with which to start the next
game.

According to John Goodwill, who supplied the above rules,
some moccasin game players possess an almost supernatural
ability to guess the location of the bead. John himself sometimes has this ability when he plays. A spark appears in his

mind's eye on these occasions, indicating the correct position
of the bead. He also used to play in concert with his uncle,
who had such supernatural power. On these occasions his uncle
would kneel beside him and John would grab four fingers of his
uncle's hand just before guessing. The finger corresponding
to the moccasin concealing the bead would tremble violently,
and always correctly.

Kenneth Eastman's account of the scoring of the game was
essentially the same as John's except in regard to the
"twelve" play. According to Mr. Eastman this play occurs when
the guesser's side has only four sticks remaining. If he hits
the bead the first time under these circumstances, his side
receives six counters. If he misses, his opponents get
twelve, hence the name of the play. A coin is flipped to
start the game, the winner of the toss acquiring four sticks
for his side and the right for them to hide first. Like John
Goodwill, Mr. Eastman was firmly convinced that certain players (including himself) have supernatural power when it comes
to playing the moccasin game.

On occasion the Canadian Sioux also play the hand game. In
this game four pieces are used and they are hidden in the
hands of two of the players instead of beneath moccasins or
moccasin-shaped pads. As in the moccasin game, two sides,
often representing two reserve communities, oppose one another.
Two persons from one side are selected to hide and each is
provided with two hiding pieces. These are usually short bone
beads, one of each pair wrapped in the middle with sinew to
distinguish it from its fellow. A guesser is selected from
the other side and the game begins. After shuffling the
pieces back and forth behind their backs, the two hiders present their closed fists to the guesser.

Using a stick or an eagle feather to indicate his guess,
the guesser gestures in one of four ways: (1) to his oppo-

nents' right, indicating that he believes that the marked
pieces are in the right hands of both the hiders; (2) to the
left, indicating his guess that the marked pieces are in the
left hands of both the hiders; (3) between them, indicating
that he thinks the marked pieces are located in the hiders'
inside hands; (4) he holds the stick or feather in the middle,
indicating that he believes the marked pieces are in the
hiders' outside hands. If he guesses the location of both
marked beads the first time he wins the right for his team to
hide. If both locations are incorrect, the hiders win two
points and the right to hide again. If he has guessed one
correctly the opponents win one point and the player who was
not guessed correctly hides again. If the guesser is successful this time his side wins the privilege of hiding, but if he
guesses wrong again his side loses another point and both of
the original hiders come back into play. Twelve counting
sticks are used in this game. As in the moccasin game, counters are won initially from a pile in the middle, then from the
opposing team. Before beginning a game, each side selects a
spokesman to select hiders and guessers, and these are replaced when unsuccessful.

The above description was provided by John Goodwill and
represents the usual form of the game. He recalled another
version, however, in which only one person hid at a time. He
had seen this variant of the game only once, when the Plains
Cree chief Pasqua and his followers visited Standing Buffalo
Reserve. Mr. Goodwill believed that this may have been a Cree
version of the game used by the Sioux to favor their guests.

Social Dances

An important part of Canadian Sioux social life was, and to a
certain extent still is, social dancing. Many dances were

primarily of a religious, ceremonial, or military nature, and these will be described in Chapter 10. There are other dances, however, which are or were purely social. These dances provided young people a chance to meet and interact with members of the opposite sex, and older married people with an opportunity for jollity and relaxation. These social dances were often, but not inevitably, held in connection with the P'ejíŋ Wac'ípi 'Grass Dance', which was itself of a ceremonial and military nature. The social dances included Haŋhé Wac'ípi or Háŋ Wac'ípi 'Night Dance'; Nasdóhaŋ 'Dragging-foot' Dance, also called Round Dance; Sihásapa Wac'ípi 'Blackfoot Dance'; Wahpé P'ejúta Wac'ípi 'Tea Dance'; and Kahómni 'Turn-about' Dance.

The Night Dance involved a feast of dog soup. According to John Goodwill it was often used like the basket socials of rural whites to raise money for some worthy cause. Men and women were seated on opposite sides of the dance hall. A man, holding a bowl of dog soup, would rise from his seat and dance across the hall to where the female partner of his choice was seated. He would dance in place before her to invite her to dance. Initially affecting coyness and embarrassment, she would finally rise and dance with him, after which she must pay a small sum to share the food in the bowl. This sum was later presented to the treasurer. A woman who refused to dance and share the food after being selected risked having the dog soup poured over her head.

The choreography of the first part of the dance is a simple toe-heel left, toe-heel right, the dancer moving forward and backward facing his potential partner. Pete Lethbridge (Wood Mountain) said that a man would dance across the hall to the person he wished to dance with, back away from her, dance forward again, back away again, repeat the same thing a third time, and then on the fourth repetition she would rise and dance with him. Since several men and women were inviting and being invited at the same time, the dance involved a rank of men facing a rank of women. The final phase of the dance, once each man had secured a partner, involved a side step to the left (clockwise), the dancers, men and women interspersed, holding hands. The songs of this dance have a heavy, measured beat (see Densmore 1918:479).

The Nasdohan (Dragging-foot) Dance is also described by Densmore (1918:477). It is the Northern Plains version of what is called the Round Dance in the Southern Plains and at Taos Pueblo, and in fact the songs are so similar in structure as to indicate a generic relationship. Although primarily a women's dance, men also participate. The dancers form a large circle with the singers standing in the center. The choreography is a simple step left, close right, hence the Sioux name for the dance, which refers to the dancers dragging the right foot up to the left. Like the Night Dance, the songs have a heavy, measured beat, the first being loud, the second soft.

Archie Eagle (White Cap) noted that the words of Nasdohan songs were often humorous in nature, sometimes nonsensical. As an example he sang one song of the dance with the words, Wakpámni kiŋ oyóhe ye, which he translated as "The river has run dry." He also recalled that the Plains Ojibwas and Plains Cree Métis who fled to Montana following the second Northwest Uprising composed some excellent Round Dance songs during their stay in the United States. When some of them returned to Saskatchewan in 1903 they brought back many good Round Dance songs. He sang one of these for me. It has Plains Cree words which he was unable to translate.

John Goodwill stated that the dance came to the Canadian Sioux from the Assiniboines of the Sinta Luta Reserve, but this is questionable since the dance is widespread and seems to be quite old among the Sioux. George Bear (Birdtail) and Pete Lethbridge (Wood Mountain) also mentioned the dance, the latter terming it, in the Teton dialect, Naslóhaŋ Wac'ípi. I saw the dance performed in August 1972 by a group of dancers from Standing Buffalo Reserve, on the occasion of the visit of a group of Japanese tourists.

The Blackfoot Dance, according to Robert Good Voice (Round Plain), came to the Sioux of Saskatchewan about 1914. It was popular for a time, but died out about 1962. This dance apparently never reached the Sioux reserves in Manitoba, although I saw it, or something very much like it, performed by the Tetons at Little Eagle, South Dakota, in 1947. The dance clearly shows white influence, probably from the quadrille. It has three figures:

(1) Men and women, interspersed, face the center of the floor, hands joined and step-close to the left, as in the Nasdohan.

(2) On the second song the men choose female partners and the couples dance face to face in a clockwise circle, the men dancing backwards.

(3) On the third song the couples promenade, as in the quadrille.

The words used in Blackfoot Dance songs, like those of the Nasdohan, are often of a humorous nature. Robert Good Voice recorded the following example:

Sihásapa wawác'i ecá, aímayapi.

When I dance Blackfoot Dance, they gossip about me.

Beatrice Medicine traces the name of the dance to the Blackfoot band of Tetons at Standing Rock, some of whom also lived at Wood Mountain.

The Tea Dance is another social dance that was apparently limited to the Saskatchewan Sioux. As they performed it, the dance was not a sacred ceremony. Archie Eagle stated that men and women danced in place, bobbing up and down. Strong black tea was often served in connection with the dance, hence the name.

The Kahomni (Turn-about) Dance takes its name from a characteristic figure in the dance, corresponding to the "swing your partner" of the quadrille. It is a couples' dance, but in this case the women usually have the opportunity to choose their male partners. Dancers proceed in a circle holding one another in the skater's embrace. The male partner, who is on the outside, steps forward with his left foot, then brings the right foot up almost, but not quite, even with it. His partner mirrors this, stepping forward with her right foot and bringing up the left. In a variation of this basic step the man steps forward with the left foot, forward with the right, then backward with the left, mirrored by his partner. There is a caller for this dance who from time to time shouts Kahómni! 'Turn-about!' at which time the couples turn completely about in place, in a clockwise direction, before continuing their larger clockwise circuit.

Variations, obviously borrowed from the white man's quadrille, have the men and women separating into two long files, doubling back, then rejoining as couples; joining hands and facing the center as in the Nasdohan and sidestepping to the left; "threading the needle"; and so on.

The drum beat is a heavy accented stroke. Some songs have merely vocables or burden syllables. Others have Sioux or English words, phrased in the verbal forms of women. These lyrics are presumed to express the thoughts of lovesick women, although of course the singers are men. The Sioux find this hilarious. An excellent example of these songs was provided by Robert Good Voice (Round Plain):

> Hé hignáwat'un kta.
> T'ehíya waún ye.
> C'éya waún ye.
> Iwányanka ye.
> Unkíye yín kte.

> I will be married.
> I am in real trouble!
> I am crying all the time!
> Now think it over!
> We two will go away.

Another Kahomni song was sung by Frank Merrick (Sioux Village):

> Tók'iya tukté
> Wik'óska aíapi.
> Hemác'a sni tuwé héca.
> C'anté masíce.

> Somewhere
> They are gossiping about a girl.
> It's not me they mean.
> I am downhearted.

Frank said that when he was a young man the youths of Sioux Village would often sing this song as they rode about thé reserve on their horses in the evening.

According to Pete Lethbridge (Wood Mountain) and Jim Ferguson (Poplar, Montana) the Kahomni developed among the Sioux in the United States and reached their Canadian kinsmen during the 1930s. It remained popular in North and South Dakota and Montana until the early 1950s but now it is seen only infre-

quently in the United States. It remains popular among the
Canadian Sioux and in fact is still spreading northward in
Saskatchewan (Corrigan 1970:256). In the Prairie provinces
the dance has become a vehicle for informal courtship. Usually there is a session of Kahomni dancing following the regular
ceremonial Grass Dance each night at the large summer powwows.
These are attended exclusively by the young people of the
camp, who wear blankets both for warmth and concealment. They
dance from midnight until seven or eight the next morning.
Corrigan notes that these Kahomni sessions constitute a "major
mating period for the participants" (1970:268). This was con-
firmed by my own observations at powwows during the summer of
1972. Because of this the dance has come to have a bad reputation among the strict church-goers.

Charles Padani (Standing Buffalo) claimed that the dance is
also called Mastíŋca Wac'ípi or Rabbit Dance, although else-
where this is a distinct dance in its own right.

8. PHILOSOPHY AND RELIGION

A great amount of traditional philosophy and world view has
survived among the Canadian Sioux, and concepts that have become forgotten or attenuated among their relatives in the
United States are still vital in Canada. It is true, of
course, that not every adult Sioux can easily explain the
various aspects of traditional religion and philosophy. I
doubt that this was ever the case. Among those Sioux who are
of a reflective nature, however, the tribal intellectuals, I
found a remarkable agreement.

Sioux philosophy might be briefly characterized as follows.
The world was made by Wak'áŋ T'áŋka ('Great Spirit', God) who
placed man and all other creatures upon it. Man, the last of
Wakan Tanka's creations, was given the right to live on the
earth and to utilize the various stones, clays, plants, trees,
and animals he found there but he must never forget that these
things are also a part of nature, placed there by Wakan Tanka.
Therefore only those substances, plants, or animals that are
to be put to good use by man for purposes of survival should
be taken, uprooted, or killed. Even then, this may only be
done in a prescribed manner and after asking permission of
Wakan Tanka and also of the spiritual prototype of the substance, plant, or animal, and excusing oneself when doing so.

Beneath Wakan Tanka in the Sioux conception are a number of
lesser deities, spirits, and supernatural beings. Each of
these has a distinctive domain and attributes, and each con-
tributes to maintaining the balance of nature. A strong dual-
istic concept is evident in this. The Powers Above, including
the Thunderbirds, eagles, hawks, swans, and lesser feathered
creatures of the air, and the bison, elk, deer, bear, and

lesser hoofed and furry creatures of the land, are generally
thought to be good. They are balanced off by the Powers Below, including the Underwater Panther, Horned Snakes, and
lesser snakes and fishes, which are generally thought of as
evil. Great storms are believed to be conflicts between these
essentially opposite forces. In the Southern Plains Arts and
Crafts outlet in Fort Qu'Appelle, Saskatchewan, I saw in 1972
an oil painting by a native artist that epitomized this conflict. In a stormy sky over a vast lake a giant eagle-like
bird was portrayed, its wings outstretched. From its eyes
bolts of lightning streaked down to the turbulent waters of
the lake, striking the head of a giant Horned Snake.

Although the Sioux consider the Thunderbirds good and the
Underwater Panthers evil, they recognize that both qualities
are inherent in nature and in man. Something good, when carried to excess, becomes harmful; likewise, even disasters and
catastrophes often have some beneficial effects. Both qualities, like positive and negative electrical charges, are
necessary components in a balanced universe. Thus, with the
Sioux, it was the Underwater Panthers, the chiefs of the Powers Below, who gave the people the Medicine Dance, and who
taught them the use of medicinal herbs (cf. Howard 1960e).
Other essentially malevolent creatures, such as the Little
Tree Dweller, can confer great power for good if approached in
the correct manner.

Each of the animal species also had its spiritual prototype
that would sometimes appear to fasters seeking visions and re-
ward them with power for war or curing. Such power, however,
was always accompanied by rules and restrictions that limited
its employment. The flaunting of these rules often led to
the power being turned back on the holder, injuring him or
some member of his family. Each individual Sioux is person-

ally responsible for maintaining the balance of the world. To
kill animals, birds, or fish for food is necessary and correct, but to kill in anger or to lose one's temper and abuse
animal life upsets the world balance and will bring retribu-
tion upon the offender or his family. This concept is exemplified in the following story told by John Goodwill (Standing Buffalo):

> One time a few years back some of us were fish-
> ing with nets out on the lake here. A jack [north-
> ern pike] was tangled in the net and one man, in
> attempting to free it, put his hand where the fish
> could bite it. Now these fish have three rows of
> teeth, all turning inward, so he had a hell of a
> time getting the fish to turn loose. He put the
> fingers of his other hand in the fish's eyes, but
> that didn't do any good. Finally he grabbed an
> ax to chop the jack from his hand. Finally it
> turned loose, but the man lost his temper and
> kept on chopping the fish until it was chopped in-
> to tiny pieces. Other Indians who were there told
> him to stop or the fish tribe would be offended,
> but he said, "It's only a fish."
> Well, when his wife was trying to deliver their
> first son she had a lot of trouble. She was in
> labor such a long time that they called in the
> Indian doctor. He is a Heyoka and was there to
> scare the baby out. His treatment worked, but the
> baby was born blind, just like the father had
> blinded that jackfish. You have seen that man.
> He is blind but he plays the accordian.

One of the principal religious symbols of the Sioux, a
symbol that illustrates the completeness and interrelatedness

of all things in nature, is the hoop or circle. Sam Buffalo
(Round Plain) commented:

> The circle is the most wakan design of my people.
> It reflects the way we do things. My people dance
> in a circle. They used to camp in a circle with
> the t'iyót'ipi ['soldier lodge'] in the center.
> Indians always sit in a circle when they are coun-
> ciling or even just visiting. One time I bet a
> white friend that if we came to the pulp mill [in
> Prince Albert] at lunch time we would find the
> Indian workers sitting in a circle. Sure enough,
> there they were, in a circle, and I won my bet.

Another important Sioux symbol is the Greek (equal-armed)
cross. This symbolizes the four winds or directions, the
corners of the universe. Each point of the cross has its own
color symbol, white for north, red for east, yellow for south,
and blue or black for west. Each of the two arms of the cross
is also symbolic. The arm extending from east to west is
called the c'aŋkú dúta, the 'red road', the path of good.
The arm extending from south to north is the c'aŋkú sápa, the
'black road', the path of war and calamity (Robert Good Voice
and Sam Buffalo; also cf. Neihardt 1961:29). Both roads are
traveled during life, and although the red road is the better
and the preferred path, the warrior must travel the black road
to protect his family and tribe.

The cross may be superimposed upon the circle to produce a
characteristic Sioux design called the c'aŋkdéska wak'áŋ
'sacred hoop', called the "medicine wheel" in English. Fur
covered hoops are sometimes carried by dancers as symbols of
the medicine wheel, and small versions, cut from rawhide and
wrapped with quillwork, are often worn as hair ornaments or

tied to deer tail "medicince brushes" attached to Grass
Dancers' deer hoof bandoliers.

The Sioux have many forms of prayer, ranging from the self
torture of the Sun Dance and Vision Quest to offering tobacco
smoke or simply raising the hand to the heavens while praying
aloud. Robert Good Voice (Round Plain) told how his grandmother had taught him to pray when he was a small child:

> My grandma would take me out in our garden and
> we would stand in the midst of all those growing
> things. She would hold my hand and raise her other
> hand to the rising sun and pray. I still do this.
> I am baptized a Catholic but I don't believe in it.
> I believe in this old Indian way of praying.

George Bear (Birdtail) mentioned that the Sioux often made
and set up waúŋyaŋpi 'offerings', referred to in English as
"medicine flags," which were prayers of thanksgiving to God.
He did not supply details but Gilmore (1919:87), quoting J.R.
Walker, described them as follows:

> Sprouts or young growths of the wild plum are
> used by the Teton Dakota in making wau^{n}ya^{n}pi. This
> is an offering or form of prayer, consisting of a
> wand, made preferably from a wild plum sprout
> peeled and painted. If painted, the design and
> color are emblematic. Near the top of the wand is
> fastened the offering proper, which may take the
> form of anything acceptable to the higher power.
> A small quantity of smoking tobacco is an article
> frequently used for this purpose. No matter how
> small a portion of the thing offered is used, the
> immaterial self of the substance is in it. Such
> offerings are usually made for the benefit of the

sick. Wauⁿyaⁿpi may be made by anyone at any
place if done with appropriate ceremony, but the
most efficient procedure is to prepare an altar
with due ceremony and there set the wand upright
with the offering fastened near the top.

Supernatural Beings

The chief of the Powers Above is Wakíŋyaŋ, the Thunderbird,
which is thought of as a giant eagle or hawk-like bird. The
flapping of its wings is the sound of thunder and the flashing
of its eyes is lightning. It is generally benevolent since it
brings the rain, but is possessed of such power that sometimes
it brings destruction. For this reason many Canadian Sioux
have on hand a supply of wac'áŋǧa 'sweetgrass', in the form of
dried braids. They burn one before a thunderstorm since the
smell of sweetgrass smoke is thought to be pleasing to the
Thunderbird and will make the storm less violent. Burning
sweetgrass in this manner was a common accompaniment to most
religious ceremonies and was also considered a deterrent to
influenza. Arthur Young (Oak Lake) gave me a braid of sweetgrass at our first meeting to be used for this purpose.

George Bear (Birdtail) recalled an episode in which a woman was burning sweetgrass to please the Thunderbird but lightning struck her house anyway, setting it afire. After this
she no longer believed in the efficacy of this procedure.

The Thunderbird, as chief of the Powers Above, is the dead-
ly enemy of the Underwater Panthers and Horned Snakes, the
chiefs of the Powers Below. The Thunderbird is worshipped in
many ceremonies, but principally in the Sun Dance. In this
ceremony, now obsolete among the Canadian Sioux, the dance
lodge was built to resemble the Thunderbird's nest, and at the
top of the center pole an extra large waúŋyaŋpi, called the

"Thunderbird's nest," was tied. The dancers in the Sun
Dance, with their half-naked costume and continual piping on
eagle bone whistles, are said by some to imitate baby Thunderbirds.

Closely associated with the Thunderbird is the Heyoka, the
anti-natural god. Individuals who dreamed of the Thunderbird
or were visited by the Thunderbird while on the Vision Quest
usually felt that they must join the Heyoka cult or society of
Clowns. This entailed appearing at least once a year at a
Grass Dance or other public gathering dressed in a ragged costume, with a mask made from a cow's paunch with small, cut-out
eye holes and a large pointed nose. Usually jagged red
streaks, symbolizing lightning, extended from the eyes down
the cheeks. The Heyoka often carried crooked bows and arrows
when they appeared at dances, in order to "shoot snakes."
They moved in a strange, backward manner, and were regarded
with a mixture of humor and fear. Some were thought to have
curative powers. Should an individual dream of the Thunderbird and not undertake to act out his dream by dancing as a
Heyoka within a reasonable time, he was said to invite being
struck by lightning.

Just as the Thunderbird is chief of the Powers Above, so
the Uŋktéhi or Underwater Panthers are chiefs of the Powers
Below. According to Robert Good Voice (Round Plain) the
Uŋktéhi are everlasting. They live in the sea, toward the
rising sun. One is an old man and one is an old woman. In
appearance they are giant panthers with horns. Mr. Good Voice
stated that it was the Uŋktéhi who gave the Medicine Dance to
the Sioux and showed them the good red road.

The Wabdúska or Horned Snakes are of lesser rank among the
Powers Below. They are conceptualized as giant horned snakes,
and live deep in the waters of lakes and rivers. Occasionally

they catch and drown a boatman or swimmer. John Goodwill commented, "Something breaks open the ice on the lake [Fishing
Lakes] even yet. There seems to be a hollow place under the
lake. We call it Táku Wak'áŋ ['Something Holy']. I suppose
it is the Wabdúška. One time lightning struck this place and
it caved in. A rotten smell was noticed in the area for
months afterward." The last remark refers to the perennial
struggle between the Powers Above and the Powers Below.

According to Robert Good Voice and Sam Buffalo (Round
Plain) Wíŋyaŋ Núŋpapi 'Double Woman' is usually a benevolent
deity. She is conceptualized as a woman with a face on both
the front and the back of her head, and is possessed of an
ability to stretch her body to enormous lengths. She has an
unearthly cry--an eldritch, shrill call resembling a woman's
laugh. Both women and men might dream of Double Woman or see
her when walking alone in the forest, but she remained invisi-
ble to all except those to whom she wished to reveal herself.

To dream of Double Woman was to have a vision conferring
unusual skill. Sam Buffalo stated that one person who had
dreamed of Double Woman invented the swing (hóhotena), both
the hammock used by the Eastern Sioux for infants and the
full-sized swing used by young people for recreation. Another
Double Woman dreamer invented the craft technique of finger
weaving, used by the Santees to make sashes, kneebands, and
turbans. Sam remembered a male Double Woman dreamer from
Round Plain, a man named Alex Swift Hawk, who died in 1964.
He possessed a medicine hoop that had a trade mirror fastened
in the center. He used this medicine hoop to find coins that
people had thrown into the brush while he was blindfolded. It
operated something like a metal detector, leading him directly
to the spot. Kenneth Eastman (Oak Lake) said that women who
dreamed of Double Woman usually became good craftworkers. He

remembered one at Sioux Valley who was partially paralyzed, yet could do many things that normal women could not.

A prominent religious cult surrounded C'aŋót'idaŋ (also called C'aŋót'ina 'Little Tree Dweller' or Woods Elf. Generally considered malevolent, he is conceptualized as a small green man, about eight inches in height, with horns on his head. He appears to solitary hunters and addresses them in a sort of double-talk. If they are foolish enough to reply, when they return to camp they will find that one of their loved ones has died. The Little Tree Dweller also causes hunters to lose their way or spoils their luck. Should a hunter happen to come up behind the elf, however, and capture it, it will trade hunting prowess for its freedom.

Charles Padani (Standing Buffalo) termed the elf "a dangerous little fellow," and stated that he lived in a hollow tree. If one tries to cut down the tree he will die. Some men, however, could overcome the elf and get power from him. These people could cure the sick using a medicine sweat bath (Inipi).

Emma Pratt (Sioux Valley) reported that some boys from that reserve saw the Little Tree Dweller as recently as 1969. They described it only as a "little green man."

Certain Sioux men and women possessed images of the Little Tree Dweller. Sam Buffalo (Round Plain) recalled seeing one formerly present on his reserve. He described it as carved of wood and fitted with blue trade beads for eyes. Kenneth Eastman (Oak Lake) described seeing such an image as well:

> I saw a C'aŋót'idaŋ doll once. It was up at
> Sioux Valley. At powwow time an old woman, who
> lived alone by herself in a little house, was mur-
> dered. Her throat was cut. A committee, of which
> I was a member, examined her house, looking for a

motive or clue as to her murderer. We thought it
might have been done for money, as she was supposed to have a bag of silver dollars. We looked
into her wópʻiye ['medicine bundle'] and found a
Little Tree Dweller doll. It was in a little
wooden container full of wahíŋjice ['downy feathers']. We didn't find any money, but on the second day of the investigation a purse was found
with new money in it. It was very wakan.

Mr. Eastman had heard that in the ceremony held for the
Little Tree Dweller the doll comes out of his "house" and
dances. Jim Kiyewakan (Sioux Valley) said much the same
thing, recalling that his mother, a Wahpekute medicine woman,
would sometimes cook tipsinna for her image of the Little Tree
Dweller. This pleased him and he would dance.

The most complete account of the Little Tree Dweller ceremony was provided by Robert Good Voice, who had seen the ceremony at Round Plain years ago. According to his account,
cloth and food offerings were displayed on an altar. A small
pit was dug before the doll owner and the doll was placed in
it. At midday the doll would come out of the pit. Turning
slowly, it finally fixed its gaze on one of those present at
the ceremony, then went out of sight again. This indicated
that something significant was going to happen to the person
thus singled out. (For a Yanktonai variant of this ceremony
see Howard 1955a.)

Of all the animals the Sioux believed to possess and to be
able to confer medicine power, the grizzly bear ranked first.
The following story, told by Jim Kiyewakan (Sioux Valley),
illustrates the way in which the Sioux regarded this powerful
animal:

One time when we were in Montana my mother and
my aunt were picking berries. A grizzly bear saw
them and came to where they were. It appeared so
suddenly that they had no chance to escape. The
bear walked up close to them but did not attack.
Instead it walked in a circle around them, standing up at each of the four directions--north, east,
south, and west. Then it slowly walked away. This
was a marvelous occurrence, and my aunt believed
that the bear gave her some of his power by doing
this. Later, when she had to swim a river with
her child on her back to escape from the enemy,
she said it was her bear power that enabled her to
do so.

So great was the belief in bear power that it might be
turned to advantage in time of war. Eli Taylor (Sioux Valley)
told a story in which this occurred:

One time a party of Dakota attacked an enemy war
party. The enemy were outnumbered pretty badly
and the Dakota succeeded in killing all of the
enemy except for one man. This man had a medicine
bundle on his back which seemed to protect him from
their arrows. This man took refuge in a thicket of
chokecherry bushes. In this thicket he found
another occupant, for a grizzly bear had made its
den there. Somehow the bear accepted the man with
the bundle and let him into his den. When the Dakota warriors would approach the bear's den the
bear would charge out and in this way the bear
killed several men and horses. The Dakota thought
it was the enemy who had changed himself into a
grizzly.

Another dimension of contemporary Canadian Sioux religious belief is the incorporation of obviously non-Sioux elements into Sioux tradition. The following legend, told by Jim Kiyewakan (Sioux Valley), is representative of this trend toward cultural syncretism. Although set in the period before white contact, the story exemplifies the great changes that have taken place in Sioux culture in the past two centuries of contact with European-derived culture.

A Miraculous Meeting

Once in the t'iyót'ipi ['soldier lodge'] the headman asked, "How big is the world?" No one knew. Therefore twelve young warriors were sent out to learn how big it was. They traveled far to the south. Finally they came to a hill. At this hill they saw a man creating horses. He had a fire and from time to time he threw powder into the fire. Each time he did so there was an explosion, and a number of young horses appeared.

Finally this wonder-worker saw the young Dakota warriors watching him. He called to them, "Don't be afraid. I made these for you." He then gave each of them a colt. He instructed them as to how they should care for these horses. Above all, he said, "Don't hit them in the face." He also gave them an herb medicine. He said, "You must fumigate your medicines from time to time and pray [i.e., perform the Medicine Feast]. Ask God what you want." This same man also taught them the use of tobacco and gave them a supply. The Dakota have wondered ever since who this personage was. He was of light complexion and we think he was Jesus.

Finally he asked the scouts, "Why did you come
this way?" They told him that they had been sent
to find out how big the world was. When he heard
this he said, "You had better go back home. It is
a very big world indeed. Now I must go back across
the water to teach the people of my complexion.
If they don't kill me I will come back. If they do
kill me, later on they will come and teach you what
they learned from me." All of this came true.

Folktales

Although the culture of the Canadian Sioux is gradually changing and coming more and more to approximate Canadian culture
in general, parents and grandparents still tell small children
tales involving the famous Iktómi (Uŋktómi) or Spider, the
Sioux Trickster and anti-hero. Both Kenneth and Wayne Goodwill (Standing Buffalo) said that they had been raised on
these stories, many of which point a moral or at least show
the folly of vain or intemperate behavior. Kenneth Goodwill
offered a version of the purloined feast as a typical example
of an Iktomi story. Sam Buffalo stated that Iktomi stories
are still popular at Round Plain as well.

Martha Tawiyaka (Standing Buffalo) told a classic Sioux
folktale involving two brothers, one of whom turned into a
fish as a result of eating a northern pike (t'ámahe) (cf.
Deloria 1967:6-7). The following tale, also told by Mrs.
Tawiyaka, is a good example of a moralistic folktale:

The Woman Who Changed Into A Deer

A pretty Dakota girl wanted to get water from
a certain slough near her parents' home, but they
would not let her go. Neither would they let her

go to gather firewood. One day she disappeared from camp. The chief sent out scouts to find her but after four days of search they gave up. One day thereafter her mother heard a voice outside the lodge. It cried, Iná, iná, iná ['Mother, mother, mother!']. Her mother went out and there was her daughter, but she had changed into a doe except for her face. A stag was with her. The daughter said, "This stag found me when I was lost. Now I am married to him and am one of the deer people. I will come and visit you from time to time." After four or five days she came to visit again, but then she went off permanently with the deer people. The moral of this story is that you should listen to your parents.

The Canadian Sioux, like many other North American Indian tribes, have a taboo against telling folktales in summer, believing that snakes will enter the rectum of the teller if he or she sits about telling stories during this season. This taboo undoubtedly served to keep people busy hunting and gardening rather than sitting about telling stories during the fine summer weather. On the other hand such stories served well in passing the time during the long winter evenings when the taboo was not in force.

Just as the English-speaking Canadian has certain birds saying, "Cheer up! Cheer up!" or "Whip poor Will!" so does the Sioux put phrases from his own language into the mouths of birds (cf. Howard 1966b). The meadowlark, according to Charles Padani (Standing Buffalo) says Kʼodá inícice 'Friend, times are hard!' Similarly, the red-winged blackbird is thought to say, Tuŋkʼíŋ matʼá niŋ 'I wish I would die!'

Magic

The Santees have a great reputation among other Sioux as prac-
titioners of magic. Members of the Medicine Lodge were particularly famous in this respect. The general theory of Santee magic was given by Pete Lethbridge (Wood Mountain), who is
himself a Teton:

> I heard of one medicine man who was a ḣmúġa
> ['wizard']. He had a necklace in his medicine bag
> made of human tongues. It was said that these
> ḣmúġa were Hiŋháŋ Káġapi ['owl shape-shifters'].
> They could change into an owl. They would fly to
> a scaffold where someone was buried and steal the
> corpse's tongue. They would dry these tongues and
> use them in their black magic. This one man had a
> complete necklace of these tongues to show how
> many people he had killed.
>
> If people saw an owl on a burial scaffold they
> would shoot it, as they knew it was a ḣmúġa. If
> they killed it, it would change back into its hu-
> man form before expiring.
>
> A ḣmúġa killed by throwing or blowing an animal
> claw or a piece of glass into a person's body.
> They could also use a piece of hair to make the
> person sick. Most of this black magic was done by
> the Isáŋt'i, not by the T'ít'uŋwaŋ. We call these
> people kiŋyáŋpi ['flyers'] because they can fly
> around in bird form and work their magic.

The above, of course, is the testimony of a Teton regarding
the Santees. However, I did secure some accounts of magic
from Santee informants as well. In 1958 Hector Obie (Standing
Buffalo) entertained me for several hours with tales of a

prominent Santee chief-shaman who used his shape-shifting
ability to escape from various stockades, prisons, and torture
chambers during the Minnesota Uprising. Jim Kiyewakan (Sioux
Valley) stated that his own great-grandfather could change
himself into an owl and fly to kill distant enemies. This is
the origin of his family name, Kiyéwak'aŋ 'Flies Holy'. This
man could also change himself into a bear or a flying squir-
rel. The Nebraska Santees tell similar stories of how certain
shamans with such power escaped from the prison stockade at
Fort Thompson, South Dakota, by changing themselves into
birds.

Another magical feat of the Santees was walking on fire.
Charles Padani (Standing Buffalo) spoke of a famous Santee
fire-walker. This man, he said, first boasted that he could
perform the feat and that he would stage it for such and such
a day. A crowd gathered. The magician appeared and built a
large fire, and when it had burned down he raked the coals into a great rectangle. The man then bet some whites who were
in the crowd that he could walk through the coals barefoot.
He not only did this, but then walked back over the flaming
surface a second time, and won a large sum of money. Lowie
(1913:125-126) describes the Fire-walker's Dance (P'éta
Nasnípi Wac'ípi), which seems to be related to the above. It,
however, was a group performance.

Only one of the old shaman-magicians is still alive among
the Canadian Sioux today, or at least only one was mentioned
to me. This man, from White Cap Reserve, is now aged and in
a rest home in Saskatoon. According to Archie Eagle, this man
in his prime was a bona fide wonder-worker, possessing the
ability to make it rain. He did this several times during the
drought years of the 1930s.

Doctoring

Indian doctors, since they promoted the health and well-being of the tribe, were highly regarded. There were different types of curers, such as the p'ejúta wic'ásta 'grass roots man' or herbalist, and the wap'íye 'renewer' or shaman who combined herbal lore with therapeutic and magical techniques. Frank Merrick (Long Plain) provided an account of the traditional manner in which a Sioux youth became a healer:

How To Become An Indian Doctor

A young man asked his mother for extra moccasins. She gave them to him and he departed. He was gone eight days. He fasted the entire time. Two days he spent traveling to a lonely place, and when he arrived there he spent four more days performing the Hamdéc'iya [Vision Quest]. Then two more days were spent coming back. During the four days of his vigil he secured a vision for curing.

When he returned to the camp he was very weak, but he refused the soup offered him. He wanted to see the chief. When he arrived at the chief's house he gave the chief a plug of tobacco and said, "Boss, I want to become an Indian doctor. I want your permission."

The chief questioned him at length and ascertained that he had had a true vision. When he learned this, the chief donated a horse and had the camp crier announce the young man's name, riding around the camp at daybreak for four mornings.

Shortly after this a man came to the young man's lodge with three yards of print cloth. He said, "My wife is sick. Here are your wages. Come and

doctor her!" The young man answered, "I'll be
there tonight. Prepare a birchbark torch so I can
see to work."

That night he appeared and doctored the sick
woman with a rattle [for diagnosis] and herbs [for
the actual cure] for four days. She recovered.
All he got was three yards of print, worth about
thirty cents. What would a white doctor have
charged?

Most middle-aged and older Sioux, even today, have some
knowledge of traditional herbal remedies. Small bunches of
dried herbs were hanging in the entryways of several homes I
visited in 1972. There is a definite procedure to be followed
in gathering medicinal herbs. Only that part to be actually
used should be taken, the rest should be put back into the
hole from which the plant was uprooted. Martha Tawiyaka
(Standing Buffalo) said that she always put a small amount of
tobacco in the hole as well. Robert Good Voice (Round Plain)
said that a person with knowledge of medicinal herbs should
share this knowledge freely with the community, not sell it.
He does this, he said. It is evident, however, that herbal-
ists sometimes gained a sizeable supplementary income from
their knowledge.

The following are a few of the herbal compounds known to
and used by the Canadian Sioux.

C'aŋnákpa 'tree ears' is a term used for several fungi, but
usually it refers to tuckahoe, the storage body or resting
place of the mushroom-like fungus Polyporus. The tuckahoe is
found in the earth, and in the Prairie provinces is often encountered when clearing poplar groves. White people mistake
it for pemican buried and forgotten by Indians. It is a
gray, spongy material, much like papier-mache in texture.

Martin Bear (Birdtail) said that cannakpa when used together
with the buffalo berry (Lepargyrea argentea [Nutt.] Greene),
provided a good treatment for itching skin. The leaves and
stems of the buffalo berry are cut up and boiled and this decoction is mixed with cannakpa that has been ground in a stone
mortar to make a salve. This treatment was also known to
Charles Padani (Standing Buffalo). George High Eagle (Oak
Lake) identified the Polyporus fungus as cannakpa and said
that it had been used by the Sioux as a food. However, he was
probably referring to Polystictus versicolor (L.) Fr., which
the Sioux also termed cannakpa. The latter is a fungus that
grows on various trees and when young and tender can be boiled
and eaten (Gilmore 1919:62).

Siŋkpét'awote 'muskrat food' is the Sioux designation for
sweet flag (Acorus calamus). Joseph Goodwill (Standing Buffalo) said that the dried rootstock of calamus is good for colds
and diabetes. Charles Padani (Standing Buffalo) also noted
its value for curing colds and sore throats. He added that
this herb is also good for dispelling ghosts. If you chew
calamus root before visiting a graveyard it makes your face
appear phosphorescent and thus repels the spirits. It is also
good for diabetes and stomach trouble. Martha Tawiyaka also
mentioned that chewing the rootstock of this plant is good for
colds and sore throat, adding that a decoction of calamus root
boiled in water, applied externally, relieves muscle ache.

P'ejúta t'ot'ó 'blue medicine' was a plant mentioned by
three informants, but I was unable to determine its botanical
identity. The flowers are said to be yellow (Martha Tawiyaka)
or bluish-green (Joseph Goodwill), and the plant is said to
stand about a foot tall. According to Mr. Goodwill, this
plant is as good as calamus root for colds and sore throat.
Charles Padani also mentioned using it for treating colds and

added that it was good for toothache as well. Martha Tawiyaka said that blue medicine should be boiled into a tea and this infusion taken by people suffering from cancer, diabetes, and tuberculosis. In cases of fever, a small piece placed under the tongue cools the body. Mrs. Tawiyaka added that the plant could be used to treat ulcers:

> A couple of years ago they told me I was going
> to have ulcers. I refused white men's medicine
> and doctored myself. I used black [blue] root
> [p'ejúta t'ot'ó] and an umbrella-shaped plant with
> many roots together with it. I call this umbrella-
> shaped plant p'ejúta ská ['white root']. It has
> many roots. When I dig it I put tobacco in its
> place. I cut up the roots, string them, and dry
> them.

C'aŋpá 'chokecherry' (Padus nana [Du Roi] Roemer), has many uses for the Sioux in addition to its food value. According to Charles Padani, the bark of the chokecherry is boiled in water to make a tea that is excellent for curing diarrhea. Martha Tawiyaka also stated that the inner bark of chokecher-ry, together with wild rose roots (uŋjíŋjiŋtka [Rosa pratin-cola Greene]), was good for burns and scabs. The rose roots and chokecherry bark are boiled together and the infusion, after it cools, is used to wash the affected area. After this treatment, c'aŋsása (Cornus stolonifera), the dried inner bark of the red osier dogwood, is powdered and put on the scab or burn. Mrs. Tawiyaka said that this treatment is also effect-ive for treating poison ivy. She also reported that choke-cherry bark, rose roots (scraped), strawberry leaves, "pinch cherry" bark [unidentified], and raspberry leaves can be brewed together to make a tea to cure diarrhea.

Icáhpe hú 'whip [?] plant' (Echinacea angustifolia DC), is the Sioux designation for the narrow-leaved purple cone flower. Charles Padani identified this as the plant used by members of the Heyoka or Clown cult when they performed Heyók'a wóze 'Heyoka dipping-in', their sacred ceremony. Members of the Clown cult acted out their visions by dipping their bare hands and arms into a kettle of boiling soup to retrieve some meat, remarking, "How cold it is!" They first bathed their hands and arms in the juice of this plant, which protected them from the heat.

Buffalo berry (Lepargyrea argentea [Nutt.] Greene) could be boiled in water and this tea mixed with a decoction from boiled Seneca root (Panax quinquefolium L.) as a cure for cholic in babies, according to Martin Bear (Birdtail).

Mr. Bear also commented that a certain brown fungus that grows eight to ten inches tall has medicinal uses. Although it is poisonous raw, the poison is dissipated when it is boiled. This fungus is brewed into a tea and administered, one spoonful per hour, to cure hiccoughs.

Another botanically unidentified plant was mentioned by Archie Eagle (White Cap). Called t'ípsiŋna iyéc'eca 'like tipsinna', it is a white root with no pronounced taste or smell. It is brewed into a tea for curing sore throat and pleurisy.

Frank Merrick (Long Plain) mentioned that lily roots, secured in Lake Manitoba (possibly Nelumbo lutea [Willd.] Pers.), are used as a medicine. Like other herbal medicines known to him, this one requires a magical phrase to activate it. Although he had been authorized by the person who told him about these roots to secure the magical phrase from a certain old woman, he had not as yet done so.

Mr. Merrick also mentioned the "smoking cure" as a therapeutic technique for a variety of illnesses. Certain medi-

cinal herbs are burned and the smoke inhaled by the patient to
effect the cure. He explained that the stones upon which the
herbs are burned must be carefully selected, and only those
from the sides of a hill can be used. Appropriate stones are
difficult to find, and when one is located, a tobacco offering must be left in its place. Mr. Merrick added that the use
of formulae or songs to activate medicines is quite common
among the Sioux, and also among their Plains Ojibwa neighbors.
For certain cures one must also burn sweetgrass and offer the
sacred pipe to the four winds, zenith, and nadir in order for
the medicine to be effective.

Mr. Merrick's second wife, a Plains Ojibwa woman from Long
Plain Reserve, had been a bleeding doctor. She would incise
a patient's temple with a piece of sharp flint, then suck out
a quantity of blood and spit it into a saucer until the blood
that came out was dark in color. Then the cure would be effective.

Mr. Merrick also mentioned the Inípi or sweat lodge ceremony as a form of therapy and ritual purification. A small
canvas-covered dome was made and a fire built outside. Four
stones were used, each carefully selected so that it would not
crack or explode. These stones were heated red hot and then
passed into the sweat lodge, one at a time, using wooden
tongs. Water was sprinkled on each stone as it was passed in
to make steam, and the stones were replaced as they cooled.
Sweetgrass was used as an aspergent. Soon the steam in the
lodge became so intense that it was all a person could toler-
ate. Mr. Merrick commented, "This is a way to get really
clean. The dirt comes right out of your pores."

Death and Burial

In their Minnesota homeland the Santees practiced both scaffold burial and interment. In Canada, only interment has been

practiced within living memory, although some of my informants had heard of scaffold burial in the past. Today each
Sioux reserve community has its own little cemetery, often
situated on a hill overlooking the settlement. A wake commonly occurs in connection with the funeral, together with a
funeral feast. Thereafter a memorial feast is held each year
at the graveside. Friends of the deceased and people of his
age group are invited to come and share a meal with the dead.
The Sioux believe that the spirit of the dead actually con-
sumes the essence of the food at these memorial feasts, while
the living guests consume the material part. On June 18,
1972, I observed this custom at Sioux Valley. Eli Taylor, the
official designated for the task, called out the names of
various individuals gathered in the parking area. Each little
group then made its way to a particular grave and there consumed food supplied by relatives of the person or persons in-
terred there.

A few weeks later, at the Sioux Valley powwow, Mr. Taylor
related the origin story of this custom:

Origin of the Memorial Feast for the Dead

Many, many years ago there were two Dakota young
men, cousins. They customarily trapped in the same
district, and camped a short distance from one
another on a lake in separate tipis with their
respective wives and children. Now it was the
custom of both of these young men, if either of
them shot a fat mallard, or trapped a fat beaver,
or killed a deer or a moose, to have his wife invite the other to a feast. As the two feasted
they would discuss their respective trap lines and
other matters. They did this for many years.

But one year one of the cousins was stricken
with a severe illness and died. The next season
the surviving cousin went to the trapping area and
established his camp there as usual. Having killed
game, he told his wife to prepare it, and, as if
his cousin were still alive, he told his wife to
set a place for him. She thought he was crazed by
grief for this dead cousin, and followed his directions.

To her amazement the figure of the deceased
cousin, dressed as in life, pushed open the tent
flap and entered, taking his seat in the accustomed place. His cousin, the inviter, chatted with
him about the placement of traps as was their
usual custom. The figure of the deceased cousin,
although he seemed to be listening, did not say
anything himself. After the meal the figure of
the deceased cousin rose and departed. It was
then that the living cousin and his wife noticed
that none of the food in his dish showed any sign
of having been touched.

The man and his wife, however, concluded that
the deceased had been present in spirit, and continued to offer such a feast for him each year
thereafter. From them, other Dakota took up the
custom, and it is still observed by Dakota people
today.

To present-day Canadian Sioux, at least those of the older
generation, the afterworld is still conceived in much the way
their ancestors thought of it. An interesting description of
the afterworld was supplied by Kenneth Eastman (Oak Lake):

A Vision of Heaven

One time when I was a boy I had double pneumonia.
I had a high fever, and in this condition I had a
vision. It seemed I was traveling down a road.
On my left hand side were grass and oak trees. On
my right hand side there were tipis and t'iúktaŋ
[domed lodges].

Four men were near one lodge. Each had a tripod
set up and they were cooking in a kettle hung on
this tripod over a fire. I called to them but
they would not look at me. All at once from one
tipi a woman emerged and began to adjust the ears
of the tipi. Suddenly I heard a woman coming toward me. She said, "What are you standing out
here for? Come inside and eat!" She extended her
hand toward me, but for some reason I did not grasp
it.

All of a sudden my ears began to ring. I opened
my eyes and I was back in my bed, at home. My dad
and mother were there, bending over me. They said,
"Are you all right?" I told them what I had experienced and they said, "You have visited heaven
and come back. It was a good thing you didn't
take that woman's hand." If I had taken her hand
I would have stayed in the land of the dead.

Now three other Indians from Sioux Valley have
experienced the same thing. Their description is
just like what I saw. Do white men ever see this?
I never heard that they do.

9. CEREMONIALISM, THE WOODLANDS HERITAGE

The Canadian Sioux possessed a rich and varied ceremonial life.
For descriptive purposes it is convenient to separate these
religious and ceremonial activities into two groupings. The
first includes those activities that the Santees share with
Woodland tribes. These include the Vision Quest, Prayer
Feast, Medicine Feast, Adoption ceremony, and Medicine Dance.
The second grouping consists of ceremonies shared by the San-
tees with High Plains groups. These include the Sun Dance,
Grass Dance and associated dances such as the Warbonnet Dance,
Heyoka or Clown cult, Horse Dance, various warrior society
dances, Scalp Dance, Ghost Dance and its derivatives, and the
Peyote religion. We cannot state with certainty that all of
the forms of this second grouping were adopted by the Santees
from western sources, although this is likely the case. Western origins are certain for the Grass Dance, Ghost Dance, and
Peyote religion, and are indicated for the Horse Dance. On
the other hand, the Sun Dance and Clown cult were present
among the Santees when they resided in Minnesota and seem to
be quite old cultural forms.

Vision Quest

The Hamdéc'iya (also called Hamdéjapi by one informant) 'crying for a vision' or Vision Quest is the Sioux version of the
custom of fasting for a vision, widespread in North America.
With the Sioux this was primarily a puberty ceremony, although
an individual might elect to perform the rite again, perhaps
several times, later in life.

The customary procedure was for the boy or man to isolate
himself in a lonely spot in the woods, on a hilltop, or even,

according to Kenneth Eastman (Oak Lake), to stand shoulder deep
in a lake. Usually, boys performing the rite for the first
time painted their faces black with soot to signal their purpose and to prevent anyone who might happen upon them from
chatting with them and thus interrupting their religious retreat. Older men performing the rite might wear special
paints and costume items relating to their earlier Wakan experiences. The individual always fasted and thirsted while
performing Hamdeciya, and prayed continually for supernatural
assistance in the form of some spiritual manifestation. The
customary time period for the rite was four days and four
nights, although some men elected longer periods. Mature
fasters sometimes carried a ceremonial pipe, which they presented stem first to the sun at dawn, midday, and sunset. If
successful, the faster would receive a vision in which an animal spirit or other spiritual manifestation would visit him,
usually in human form, and instruct him as to how and where he
might secure substances that would provide him with power or
luck in the future.

Jim Kiyewakan (Sioux Valley) mentioned that Canadian Sioux
warriors often performed Hamdeciya to secure war medicines,
particularly for use against the Plains Ojibwas and Plains
Crees. Other men prayed for a knowledge of herbal remedies.
Robert Good Voice said that a man from Round Plain Reserve
performed Hamdeciya and on the fourth day saw four plants in
his vision. He later dug these and used the roots as a medicine to cure venereal complaints.

Kenneth Eastman (Oak Lake) told an amusing tale about a man
from Carlyle, Saskatchewan (White Bear Reserve, inhabited by
Plains Ojibwas, Plains Crees, and Assiniboines) who was performing the Vision Quest on top of a hill in that area. He
was attired, as is usual for fasters, in a breechcloth and

medicine paints. He also wore, as his personal medicine garb, a headdress with bison horns. As the faster came down the hill at the end of his fourth day he encountered a white tourist who ran away screaming that he had just seen the devil!

There seems to be a connection between the Hamdeciya and the Sun Dance. Both involve fasting and thirsting and both may involve piercing the chest and other forms of self torture. More importantly, both are dedicated to the same end. The essential difference between the two is that Hamdeciya is a solitary rite while the Sun Dance is a public one.

Prayer Feast and Medicine Feast

The C'ékiya Wóhaŋpi 'Prayer Feast' seems to be a Santee form of ancient Woodland first-fruit rites, although the ritual was later blended with Ghost Dance teachings among the Saskatchewan Sioux at White Cap and Round Plain. John Goodwill (Standing Buffalo) described the older procedure:

> Suppose a young man out hunting kills a swan.
> He gives it to his relatives who prepare it for
> the feast. The young man then invites various
> people who own medicine bags [members of the Medi-
> cine Lodge] to a Cekiya Wohanpi. The medicine
> bags are collected and taken to the place where
> the feast will be held. They are lined up in a
> row on a blanket spread on the floor. A pipe is
> put in front of these medicine bags. One of the
> men is selected, when all have assembled, to be
> the spokesman [priest]. He sings and prays for
> the group. Food is offered to bless the medicines,
> which strengthens them.

The Prayer Feast seems to be closely related to, if not a variant form of, the Wak'áŋ Wóhaŋpi 'Medicine Feast', another

typically Woodland ceremonial expression of the Santees. The
Medicine Feast was held to renew the power of personal medicines (the wopiye or medicine bags and the wotawe or war medicines) according to Emma Pratt and Jim Kiyewakan (Sioux Valley), George Bear (Birdtail), Hector Obie and John Goodwill
(Standing Buffalo), Robert Good Voice and Sam Buffalo (Round
Plain) and Kenneth Eastman and Arthur Young (Oak Lake).
Robert Good Voice also stated that such a feast might be held
to end the mourning of a bereaved person. A Medicine Feast
might be staged at any time in order to strengthen the medicines, but Sam Buffalo said that autumn was the usual season.

A salient feature of the Medicine Feast was the use of
large wooden feast bowls. Such bowls, carved from elm burls,
often measured a foot or more in diameter. These usually had
a carved head at one side. Some of these carved heads represented loons, the Thunderbird, or Íya, the god of gluttony.
Brass tacks were used to indicate the eyes of these effigy
heads. A few Medicine Feast bowls are still in Indian hands
but most are now owned by white collectors.

The best description of the Medicine Feast was provided by
John Goodwill (Standing Buffalo):

> At a Medicine Feast you have to eat everything
> in your dish or pay a fine. It is said that no
> one could eat an entire moose nose singlehanded.
> If siŋkpét'awote ['muskrat food', Acorus calamus]
> was eaten before such a feast, one could consume
> a lot of grease. I did this once and managed to
> eat a huge dish of roast pork at an eat-all feast.
> I still have my old wooden bowl used by my family
> in these feasts. It has a raised part at one side,
> a sort of handle, but this is broken off. It is
> highly polished from use. Wooden spoons are used.

To invite someone to such a feast they come to
your house and take your medicine bag. Then you
have to come to the feast to get it back. Only
persons who have sponsored feasts can invite others
to a feast. This rule also applies to the servers.
A few old medicine bundles are still present on
this reserve. They are made of some kind of thick
cloth and have designs like a snake's skin [the
typical Central Algonquian twined yarn bag]. Some
have animal or bird designs in the material.

Hector Obie (Standing Buffalo) described the characteristic
eat-all Medicine Feast in 1958. He commented that he had permanently ruined his digestion by attending one of these feasts
and eating too much too quickly.

George Bear (Birdtail) said that at the Medicine Feast,
evergreen needles and sweetgrass were burned and the medicine
bags were fumigated in the smoke. Kenneth Eastman (Oak Lake)
mentioned only sweetgrass as the fumigant in the Medicine
Feasts. He commented:

> One man decides to put on the ceremony. Every-
> one brings his c'aŋwáksica ['wooden bowl']. These
> are large wooden bowls with an animal head at one
> side. The sponsor of the feast sings holy songs.
> I took part in such a feast once. One man did
> it to strengthen his hunting medicines. This was
> on a hunting trip to the Riding Mountain area.
> A lot of food was put on my plate and I could not
> eat my portion.

Most informants stressed the connection between the Medicine Feast and the Medicine Dance. The medicine bags employed
in the feast were undoubtedly the same as those used in the

Medicine Dance. Robert Good Voice (Round Plain) stated that
the "red road" was an important symbolic concept in both
rites. He commented, "This is the good path of life. One
hundred and fifty different roots are used in the various
medicines found in the medicine bags. The red path leads to
life everlasting."

The Medicine Feast was present on all eight Canadian Sioux
reserves, including Wood Mountain. Pete Lethbridge, of the
latter reserve, described a ceremony he had attended: "At
this ceremony only medicine men were invited. They all had
yarn medicine bags. These were renewed at the feast."

Adoption Feast

Another Canadian Sioux ceremony very reminiscent of the Eastern Woodlands is the Adoption Feast. These feasts are perhaps
the most common ceremonial expression of such groups as the
Kickapoos, Potawatomis, and Meskwakis. It was most interesting to find that they were also quite important to the Santees
until a few years ago. John Goodwill (Standing Buffalo) said:

> We used to have Adoption Feasts quite often, but
> they are rare now. I think the last one on this
> reserve was held five years ago [1967]. My son
> was killed when his bed caught fire. I guess he
> was smoking in bed. We adopted Sam Corrigan [an
> anthropologist] to replace my son. We had a feast
> and dressed Sam in my boy's Indian costume. This
> was the last Adoption Feast held on this reserve,
> though there have been others in the past ten
> years.

The essential features of this ceremony--the feast and the
dressing of the adoptee in the clothing of the deceased--are

the same in Kickapoo, Sauk, Meskwaki, Potowatomi, and Iroquois adoption feasts that I have observed. The giving away of the deceased's clothes is an important part of the Adoption Feast. Sam Buffalo (Round Plain) described one occasion on which the adoptee was dressed in a beautifully beaded and quilled dancing costume that had belonged to the deceased.

Medicine Dance

The Wak'áŋ Wac'ípi 'Medicine Dance' or Medicine Lodge was preeminent among the Woodland-derived ceremonial organizations of the Santees. In its essentials it is the same as the Ojibwa and Sauk Midewiwin, although it seems to have developed its own characteristically Sioux features. The Medicine Dance seems to have disappeared by the 1860s among the Santees in the United States (Skinner 1920:262), but it persisted for at least seventy years longer among the Canadian Sioux. I was able to secure good descriptions of the ceremony from Jim Kiyewakan (Sioux Valley), George Bear (Birdtail), Robert Good Voice and Sam Buffalo (Round Plain), Frank Merrick (Sioux Village), and Kenneth Eastman and Arthur Young (Oak Lake). Each of these individuals had either participated in the ceremony themselves or were familiar enough with it by having discussed it with members that they could provide detailed accounts. Arthur Young owns an heirloom photograph of the ceremony taken in 1929 or 1930, which may be the only photograph in existence of this important Santee rite. I was assured that there were still some individuals who knew the songs of the ceremony, but I was unsuccessful in my attempts to find someone willing to tape record them for me.

The Medicine Dance was highly regarded by all informants. Its members, they agreed, were "high class," religious people,

circumspect in their behavior and generous to their fellow
tribesmen. Many possessed great power. The society was composed of a number of separate groups--which my informants
called "bands"--and apparently there were at least two of
these groups present on each reserve where the ceremony was
practiced.

The ceremony was held in a brush arbor about forty feet
long and ten feet wide, rounded at the ends. This arbor was
open at the top but covered on the sides to a height of about
five feet. It was oriented east and west, with openings at
either end. At the west end, blocking the west door, a tipi
was pitched opening into the main lodge. Here the leaders of
the ceremony were seated when not otherwise engaged. A short
distance from the eastern doorway, another tipi (in later
times a wall tent) was pitched. This was the headquarters of
the akicita, a group of warriors selected to keep order in the
vicinity of the lodge while the ceremony was in progress.
These soldiers would catch, kill, and singe any dog that
strayed near the dance lodge. Because of this custom the
people in the camp were always careful to tie up their dogs
when a ceremony was in progress. A stone, shaped like an ar-
tillery shell set on end, was placed in the center of the
ceremonial lodge. This was a symbol of eternal life.

An individual joined the society by first applying to the
leader of one of the groups making up the organization. This
was done at a feast prepared by the applicant. If this leader
was favorable to the candidate another feast followed, to
which the leaders of both (or all, if there were more than
two) groups were invited. If accepted, the candidate was
given instruction and the origin legend of the society was recounted. A sweat lodge ceremony followed at which the candidate was lectured further. On this occasion he would give

valuable presents of blankets to the leaders. All information concerning the society acquired by the candidate must be paid for, even if he secured it from his own parents. Frank Merrick stated that when he joined the ceremony he put up four complete suits of clothing as partial payment to the leaders.

The regalia of the society was worn or used only during the society's rites. Each member was given a ptáŋ c'aŋtójuha 'otter tobacco bag' or animal skin medicine bag. Most were made of otter skin, but Frank Merrick mentioned that beaver, mink, and "rabbit snake [?]" bags were also used. Some of these "rabbit snake" bags were, he said, eight feet long. All the other types of medicine bags consisted of the entire tanned skin of the creature, with the skull, paws and tail left intact. The legs and tail might be decorated with quillwork or beadwork. The nasal septum of the animal was pierced and red-dyed hackle feathers were inserted in the opening. Some of the men belonging to the society wore turbans of otter skin, snake skin, or yarn sashes. The snake skin turban consisted of the entire skin of a pine snake wrapped around the wearer's head, the tail hanging down his back. Some men wore fancy capouche headdresses and other Woodland style costume pieces, usually decorated with floral beadwork. Women members always wore long dresses.

The drum used in the ceremony was a Woodland style water drum, which was beaten with an "L" shaped stick. A large gourd rattle (wakmúha) was shaken in time with the drum.

Each member of the society also had a yarn medicine bag in which his or her medicines were kept. These were not usually brought to the ceremonies. All animal skin medicine bags, yarn medicine bags, and costume items used in the Medicine Dance were kept away from women during their menstrual period, as menstrual blood was believed to destroy the power of medicine.

The first day of a Medicine Dance ceremony involved the construction of the lodge and the erection of the two tipis. That evening there was a practice singing session. On the second day the leaders of the ceremony took their places at the west end of the lodge. Then the groups making up the organization entered one at a time. As each group entered, its members formed a line at the east end, facing west. They raised their right hands in unison and sang one of their sacred songs, then marched in a clockwise direction to take their seats at one or the other side of the lodge. When all groups had been seated the ceremony proper began.

A catlinite pipe was offered to the four directions, zenith, and nadir, and then passed to those present. The drum and gourd rattle were given to one group. Four men from this group then sang while the remainder danced. When they finished there was a feast. There were four segments to the dance, the drum changing from one side of the lodge to the other, with a feast after each segment. The dance itself was a simple bobbing up and down in place. Four single beats of the drum (four being the sacred number) preceded each song.

On the final day of the ceremony, if it was an initiation rite, the famous "shooting" occurred. The candidate was seated in the center of the lodge and the membership, one person at a time, charged down at him. Each shooter held his animal skin bag extended head first toward the candidate, then stopped a short distance away and shook the animal skin in the candidate's direction, uttering the sacred cry. This was supposed to propel the "medicine arrow" (a small shell) from the bag into the candidate's body. If allowed to remain, he would supposedly sicken and die. The candidate, however, would retch violently and bring up the shell. Then the whole process would be repeated. During the medicine shooting each group shot in turn. When all had shot the candidate there was a general shooting, the initiate joining the more experienced members of the order. According to Arthur Young, some people with great power simply staggered a bit when shot. Others fell as if dead and required "doctoring" to remove the magical projectile.

This portion of the ceremony, of course, was very dramatic and attracted a great number of spectators. However, it was dangerous for nonmembers to be too near the medicine shooting, since they might accidentally be hit by one of the flying projectiles. Lacking the power to bring up the magic bullet, nonmembers might sicken and die as a result. One man from Sioux Valley, Jim Essie, was accidentally shot in this manner when he was a boy. Jim Kiyewakan recounted a famous shooting that occurred at a Medicine Dance in 1867. One member of the society, a famous shaman, shot another member using an owl claw. The man remained as dead for several days until the shooter extracted the claw and brought the victim to life again.

A man from Round Plain told Sam Buffalo that when he joined the Medicine Dance in 1914 the leaders lectured to him for an entire day about the teachings of the order. Finally, they asked him to swallow the "medicine arrow" in order to protect himself against projectiles shot at him in the ceremony to follow. In this case the medicine arrow was some down from a prairie chicken rolled into a tiny ball. In Santee belief this would gradually change into a shell. The man commented that after he had taken the pellet into his mouth, "I didn't know where [in my body] it went. It was there, though, somewhere inside me, because in 1936 I went to a Wakan Wacipi at Griswold [Sioux Valley] and in the shooting I managed to bring it up again."

In order to sing the songs of the Medicine Dance in their proper order, the singers often provided themselves with pictographic records on pieces of birchbark or small slabs of wood. According to Jim Kiyewakan, Henry Two Beard, at Sioux Valley, had such a birchbark record. The wooden slabs seem to have been more common among the Sioux, however, and several are preserved in museums in Canada and the United States. Some of the symbols used on these song records are highly conventionalized while others are symbolic representations of the animal or bird mentioned in a particular song. Sam Buffalo said that Jim Blacksmith, at Sioux Valley, is one of the few Santees who can still read Medicine Dance pictographs. Mr. Buffalo said that there are twelve initial symbols. The lightning symbol, for example, indicates voice, while the circle indicates sacred power. Magical power is thought to inhere in both the song records and the songs themselves. It is considered dangerous to the singer and listener both if the songs are sung on any occasion except at rehearsals or actual ceremonies. This probably explains why I could find no one who would admit to the knowledge of any of these songs.

Jim Kiyewakan told of a famous performance of the Medicine Dance held when some of the Sioux were living in the Turtle Mountain area in Manitoba. There was a lake nearby and the ceremony was held on its shore. The songs of the Medicine Dance were so compelling on this occasion that an elm tree nearby was observed to be "dancing," vibrating its leaves and branches in time with the music.

Sometimes at ceremonies of the order, shamans in the membership would demonstrate their power. Joseph Goodwill told of a magical performance by a Medicine Dance member. Pointing to the stone in the center of the lodge, he boasted that he would magically shoot a bear claw through it. He charged toward the stone as if it were the candidate in the shooting rite, extended his medicine bag, and stamped his foot. Spectators saw a spurt of dust from behind the stone and retrieved the bear claw. Then they examined the stone and found a small opening from which blood was slowly oozing. Mr. Goodwill said that the stone remained at the site for many years until it was finally carried off by his son Alex.

Fragments of the origin legend telling how the Sioux received the Medicine Dance were recounted by Robert Good Voice and Sam Buffalo. Mr. Buffalo stated that he had received much of his information from James Black and Willie Gunn, both Medicine Dance members. The following is a composite of Mr. Good Voice's and Mr. Buffalo's separate accounts, which complemented one another.

Origin of the Medicine Dance

Many years ago the Dakota people landed on a peninsula on the east coast of North America. They were surrounded by waters and could go no further, so they prayed. Finally, in response to their prayers, they heard a great voice, and above the surface of the ocean, in the direction of the sunrise, they saw the heads of two spirits. These were the Uŋktéȟi [Underwater Panthers]. One was male and sóta ['grayish-white'] colored. The other, a female, was the color of a buffalo calf [reddish-brown]. They were like giant panthers in shape, but had horns like a buffalo.

These spirits told the people to travel west, following the c'aŋkú dúta, the 'red road'. [In other words, to perform the Medicine Dance and to follow the teachings of the organization.] This

road, they said, has four divisions [the four
groups making up the society?]. The promise of
the red road, the U̲ŋkté̲ȟi said, is as true as what
you can see. The people looked toward the west and
saw that their path seemed to lead into the sea.
They feared that they would be drowned, but they
had faith and followed the red road.

When they came to the water, one man stepped on
it, and it parted, revealing a dry path. The rest
followed. The red road led the Dakota west to the
Minnesota country and they kept up their Wak'áŋ
Wac'ípi from that time onward. Some men here still
know the songs and we still believe in its teachings.

Animal Dreamers

In the nineteenth century the Santees possessed a number of
cults composed of individuals who had received power from
various animals, such as the elk, buffalo, and bear (Lowie
1913). Today, with their changed cultural situation, these
have disappeared. Of my Canadian Sioux informants, only
Charles Padani said that he had heard of a class of medicine
men known as the T'áȟca Wic'áša Wak'áŋ 'Deer Holy Men'. One
time an old shaman of this type spread loose dirt on the
ground and smoothed it. He then announced that he was going
to do something miraculous. He walked through this loose dirt
and left four deer hoofprints. This same man could accurately
predict through his deer power the coming of winter and of
spring. He also had the power to call the deer to the hunters
with a sacred song. "There are no men with such power today,"
Mr. Padani commented in concluding his account.

10. CEREMONIALISM, THE PLAINS HERITAGE

Those ceremonials of the Canadian Sioux that they shared with
Prairie and High Plains tribes include the Sun Dance, Grass
Dance and associated dances, Heyoka or Clown cult, Horse
Dance, various warrior society dances, Scalp Dance, Ghost
Dance, and Peyote religion. The Vision Quest, described in
the previous chapter, was practiced by both Woodland and
Plains groups, as was the Scalp Dance, although the Canadian
Sioux form of the latter seems to share more traits with the
Plains than with Woodland forms of the dance.

Sun Dance

The Sun Dance, as of 1972, was no longer practiced by the Canadian Sioux as a tribal ceremony on any reserve, although it
was still vital to the Plains Ojibwas, Plains Crees, and Assiniboines, all of whom either received the dance directly
from the Sioux or were strongly influenced by the Sioux form
of the ceremony. Why they should continue the ceremony after
their teachers abandoned it is an interesting problem in cultural dynamics. A few Canadian Sioux at the present time attend and have participated in the Plains Cree Sun Dance, but
always as individuals. I heard no talk of reviving the Sioux
form from my informants.

All of my older informants who had seen the Sioux Sun Dance
described it as more difficult than the Plains Cree version.
Thus Jim Kiyewakan (Sioux Valley) remarked: "We Dakota gazed
at the sun all day long, which was hard to do. The Cree just
gaze at the Thunderbird's nest." Robert Good Voice (Round
Plain) commented: "In the old time Sun Dance they actually
watched the sun. The Powers Above gave certain men instruc-

tions and they became leaders in the Sun Dance. Even trees and stones gave instructions. In this dance we never prayed with empty pipes." The Sioux name for the dance, Wiwáŋyaŋke Wac'ípi 'Sun Gazing-at Dance', would seem to bear out these statements.

The Sun Dance, including the Canadian Sioux form, has been fully described (Wallis 1919). Briefly, the ceremony was undertaken by a pledger, who might be assisted by others or dance alone. It was usually held in June or July. The lodge, erected on the first day of the ceremony, was a circular brush arbor, in the center of which a tall, forked pole was erected, with a number of plum branches and cloth banners attached at the fork. This pole with its bunch of plum brush, and in fact the entire Sun Dance lodge, represented the nest of the Thunderbird, to whom the dance was dedicated. The men dancers were naked except for a red deerskin kilt and breechcloth and their sacred ornaments. These ornaments included a chaplet of sage with horn-like feathers projecting at the sides and scratching sticks attached at the back. They wore their hair loose and unbraided. Other ornaments included wristlets of sage and rabbit fur anklets. Around the neck, on a cord, each carried an eagle bone whistle upon which he piped while dancing. Offerings, carried in the hand, included cloth banners and wreaths of sage. Some dancers wore otter skin neckpieces with rawhide cutouts resembling sunflowers. These symbolized the fact that the dancer, like the sunflower, followed the sun with his gaze. Women dancers wore long white dresses of tanned buckskin or cloth, and like the men, the sage chaplet and whistle about the neck. The dance was a simple bobbing up and down in place, although occasionally a dancer or a group of dancers would advance toward the center pole, then retreat. The dancers, in their unusual costumes, constantly piping on their whistles, are said by some to be imitating baby birds, pleading for their mother (the Thunderbird) to come and bless them.

Dancers thirsted and fasted during the entire dance, which usually lasted four days and three nights. On the last day of the dance special torture vows were fulfilled. Peter Lethbridge (Wood Mountain) commented:

> On the last day the chest of the dancer was
> pierced with a bone knife and he would "pull the
> rope." Skewers were inserted in his chest in the
> openings made by the bone knife and these attached
> with rawhide thongs to a rawhide rope attached
> high on the center pole. Sometimes a dancer would
> say, "I am going to pull the rope for fifty songs."
> He would then begin to dance, leaning backward on
> the rope so that it pulled on his chest muscles
> where the thongs were attached to the skewers. At
> the end of fifty songs his flesh would be cut and
> he would be released. Or he might say, "I am go-
> ing to dance until I pull myself loose." Then he
> would continue until the flesh broke from his pull-
> ing on the rope. Again, some dancers would pledge
> to drag buffalo skulls, in which case slits were
> made in the flesh of their back and they would
> attach thongs, threaded through these slits, to
> heavy bison skulls and drag them around the lodge.

Generally a man would pledge during midwinter to perform the Sun Dance, asking Wakan Tanka to cure a sick wife, child, or other relative, offering his participation in a specified form of the dance in exchange for the cure. Formerly a warrior might pledge the dance in return for an enemy scalp to

avenge the death of a relative. Sun Dance priests, men who
had performed the dance many times and were selected by nov-
ices as their teachers, would sometimes perform magical acts
during the dance to demonstrate their power. Jim Kiyewakan
recalled such a man who, noting that the dancers were suffering excessively from their abstention from water, cut spiral
strips of bark from the center pole of the lodge. Then, using
two eagle wing fans, he danced imitating the Thunderbirds and
sang. Water began to trickle down the spiral incisions and
dripped into a bowl. He then gave each of the dancers a
swallow from this.

Frank Merrick (Long Plain) told of attending a Plains Ojibwa Sun Dance at Swan Lake Reserve in Manitoba. It was very
hot and the dancers were dry. A man came to Mr. Merrick's
camp and borrowed a pail. He took this back into the Sun
Dance lodge. The man prayed with the sacred Sun Dance pipe
and sang a special song. In about an hour a thunderstorm
came. It began to rain heavily but people kept on dancing.
The pail was placed near the center pole, and soon it was
full. The dancers were given a drink from this.

The Sun Dance seems to have been abandoned on most Sioux
reserves by 1910. Archie Eagle (White Cap), who is 65 years
old, said that it had not been performed on his reserve during
his lifetime. Jim Kiyewakan, age 72 (Sioux Valley), had seen
it as a child, as had Charles Padani, age 65 (Standing Buffalo). Robert Good Voice stated that a Sun Dance had taken
place near Prince Albert in 1962. This is probably the dance
mentioned by Kehoe (1970:163), which was sponsored by a middle-aged half-Sioux, half-Cree man from Round Plain who
dreamed that the Thunderbird ordered him to sponsor the dance
for the health of his family. According to Kehoe he fulfilled
this vision by inviting Plains Cree ritual leaders to perform
the Thirsting Dance, the Plains Cree version of the Sun Dance.

Horse Dance

The Horse Dance, sometimes held in connection with the Sun
Dance, was described by Emma Pratt (Sioux Valley) and by
Joseph Goodwill and his son John Goodwill (Standing Buffalo).
Like the Sun Dance, the Horse Dance was pledged by a person
seeking some benefit for himself or a member of his family.
John Goodwill stated:

> We used to have the Horse Dance on this reserve.
> The place they have it must be a place not fre-
> quented by women. Wild [unbroken] horses were
> rounded up and chased into a corral. Here they
> were painted and decorated by tying feathers into
> their tails. A man prayed and sang for the dance.
> He had a little lodge made of branches stuck into
> the earth. This was in the center of the dance
> arena. The Wakan thing about this dance was that
> the horses kept time to the music.

Joseph Goodwill said that twelve boys were involved in the
dance as riders. Six of them rode grays and six rode blacks.
He also mentioned that the horses kept time to the music.
John Goodwill recalled seeing a Plains Cree version of this
dance at Poorman's Reserve. A small boy was ill, so the boy's
father pledged the dance if the Powers Above would make the
boy well enough to ride. Poplar trees were placed in a circle
and their tops were tied together to form a dance lodge. On
the south side two or three poplar trees were erected, and
ponies were tied to them. The pledger painted the horses and
helped his son to mount. One other boy, a friend of the sick
boy, rode as well. As the musicians sang, the boys rode
around the lodge. In this Cree version, as in the Sioux Horse

Dance, the horses were observed to dance to the music. Like the Sun Dance, the Horse Dance is now obsolete among the Canadian Sioux, although it is still practiced by the neighboring Plains Crees and Plains Ojibwas.

Warrior Society Dances

In his "Dance Associations of the Eastern Dakota" (1913), Lowie describes a number of Santee warrior dancing societies and religious cults. The warrior dancing societies include the Kit Fox, No Flight, Raven Owners, Badger, Owl Feather, and Elk Ear societies. Of these, Jim Kiyewakan (Sioux Valley) remembered only the No Flight and a nearly identical dance called the Strong Heart. Charles Padani (Standing Buffalo) remembered the same two, but called the latter "Black Stone Heart." Archie Eagle (White Cap) also recalled the No Flight dance.

Members of the No Flight (Nap'éšni) and Strong Heart (C'aŋté T'íŋza) dance societies wore headdresses consisting of buckskin skull caps covered with fringes of ermine skin. At the sides, split, curved buffalo horns were attached, and beneath them were bunches of owl feathers. At the back was a feathery rudder of black and white eagle feathers. Some of the members carried ring-shaped rawhide rattles and straight lances; the latter were each decorated with a row of eagle feathers attached to a sleeve of red strouding that extended the length of the lance. In their dance the members of the society bobbed up and down in place at the beginning of the song, then took a few steps forward on musical cue, stopped, and bobbed up and down again. The dance would seem to be a cognate of the One-legged Dance of the Plains Ojibwas and the Gourd Dance of the Southern Plains tribes in Oklahoma (see Howard 1976).

The name No Flight refers to the fact that members of this dancing society, when they went into battle, did not retreat before an enemy attack, but stood their ground. The name Strong Heart has a similar connotation, while Charles Padani's variant name, "Black Stone Heart," referred to the fact that the society was composed of men "who were so brave that they did not take any notice even if someone stole their wife." This last statement probably indicates that wife stealing, of the type so well known among Crow warrior societies, was also practiced by the Sioux.

Another Santee society, apparently of the same type as the above, was the Brave Dance (Ohítika Wac'ípi). It was mentioned by Robert Good Voice (Round Plain) and Charles Padani (Standing Buffalo), both of whom noted that it was an old warrior dance. Charles Padani said that the society possessed medicine that served to make its members brave.

Jim Kiyewakan (Sioux Valley) mentioned a group called the Duck (Maǧáksica) society. It was composed of warriors and a feature of its performance was a feast in which the members ate a duck without benefit of bowl or spoon, each warrior ripping a bite of meat from the duck with his teeth. This feature is very reminiscent of the Raw Fish Eaters and Dog Liver Eaters dances described by Lowie (1913:123-125).

Only Pete Lethbridge (Wood Mountain) recalled the Kit Fox society, which he called, in the Teton dialect, T'okála Wac'ípi ('Kit Fox Dance'). He had seen the dance as a boy, and noted that the men danced in place, gradually turning during the song. Jim Ferguson (Poplar, Montana), who was present when Mr. Lethbridge spoke of the Kit Fox Dance, mentioned a Coyote Dance, which may be related. He said:

One time the Dakota people had been traveling. They decided to stop and camp at a certain place.

As they approached this camping spot they heard beautiful singing. They sent out scouts, but all the scouts could find was an old, starving, flea-ridden coyote. He had been singing and they learned his song.

Grass Dance

As can be seen from the above, information on warrior society dances to be recorded among the Canadian Sioux today is very sketchy. The dances passed from use so many years ago that their characteristic costumes, songs, customs, and dance choreography are largely lost. One warrior society dance, however, continues to be popular with the Canadian Sioux. Its form and function have changed through the years but the distinctive elements of its costume and its characteristic music are still vital. This dance, originally of the warrior society type, is the P'ejíŋ Wac'ípi 'Grass Dance', also called Heyúska (from the Omaha-Ponca name Hethúska). Lowie (1913: 130) notes that the Santees in the United States also called this Hot'áŋka Wac'ípi 'Winnebago Dance'. Wallis (1947:50) was told that the Wahpetons received this dance from the Winnebagos in 1847 or 1848. Teton Sioux winter counts indicate that they received the dance from the Omahas or Poncas (the Sioux call the two tribes by the same name, Omáha) in the early 1860s (see Howard 1960c, 1960d, 1968). The name Omáha Wac'ípi 'Omaha Dance', is used for this dance by the Tetons at Wood Mountain, and is a variant name at Standing Buffalo.

There were two forms of the dance, the P'ejíŋ T'áŋka 'Big Grass', and P'ejíŋ Hoksína 'Young Men's Grass'. The former type was customarily held twice a year, in the spring and fall. It involved several ritual acts that were not present in the Young Men's Grass Dance. The Big Grass Dance is now

obsolete, although I secured excellent descriptions of it from
Robert Good Voice (Round Plain), Jim Kiyewakan (Sioux Valley),
Arthur Young (Oak Lake), John Goodwill (Standing Buffalo), and
Pete Lethbridge (Wood Mountain). Robert Good Voice, John
Goodwill, and Pete Lethbridge also recorded the ritual songs
of the dance, in sequence. There were slight variations in
the ceremonial procedures recorded at each reserve. In view
of the great importance of the dance to the Sioux and the
general interest in it, I will present each of these variants
in turn after discussing some general features common to all
and giving an idealized reconstruction of an old time performance. (Compare the account of the Assiniboine Grass Dance
given by Long [1961:125-50].)

The choreography of the Grass Dance, which is the same for
the Big Grass and the Young Men's Grass, is distinctive and
exciting, even for the outsider who cannot appreciate the
finer points. Each dancer moves as a unit, gliding forward,
occasionally whirling in place or shaking the shoulders, but
always strictly in time to the singing and beating of the big
drum, and always stopping precisely on the last beat of each
song. Generally a simple toe-heel left, toe-heel right step
is employed, but skilled dancers perform infinite variations.
The general line of direction of the dance is clockwise.
Formerly, women and girls were excluded. This was probably a
general rule for the Big Grass form, but since about 1920 wom-
en have been admitted. Their movements are generally more
stately and reserved than those of the men, although since
about 1965 some young women have begun to dance in the men's
fashion.

Since the Big Grass Dance, the formal version of the dance,
is basic and since some of its features survive in attentuated
form in the secularized Young Men's Grass Dance, I will begin

the consideration of the Grass Dance complex with it. Like
the other warrior dancing societies of the Santees discussed
earlier, the Grass Dance was originally limited to men, and
like those other societies its members went into battle wearing the regalia of the society, particularly the porcupine and
deer hair roach headdress and the feather dancing bustle or
"crow belt."

Lists of officers of the society differ from one reserve
group to another, likewise from one informant to another. The
following is a composite drawn from several accounts:

     1 drum keeper

     1 drum warmer

     1 announcer

     2 waiters or servers

     1 big forked spit carrier

     1 spoon carrier

     1 "wounded warrior"

     4 male singers, one of whom was designated head
       singer

     4 female singers

     2 whip carriers

     1 "enemy warrior" who carried a red-painted
       wooden gun

     x lay members (usually 20-30)

Of these officers the two waiters, the big forked spit carrier, the spoon carrier, and the "wounded warrior" were entitled to put on and wear, at prescribed times, the ornament
called k‘aŋgíha miknáka 'crow skin tucked in' or crow belt.
This was a type of bustle worn at the level of the hips in
back, held up by a Hudson's Bay Company yarn sash. It consisted of a rawhide "pillow" at the top of which two eagle
wing feather "pointers" were attached so as to stand upright

or project backward. Beneath these, and hanging down almost
to the wearer's heels, were pieces of heavy red or blue Hudson's Bay Company stroud cloth to which eagle tail feathers
were fastened so as to flutter gracefully when the wearer
danced forward. The feathers of one of the five crow belts
used by the society were dyed red. This belt was worn by the
"wounded warrior," a position traditionally filled by a man
who had been wounded in combat. These crow belts, with the
Sioux and neighboring tribes, were symbolic of the Thunderbird, the guardian of warriors. Like the Sun Dance, the Grass
Dance was dedicated to the Powers Above. Formerly these crow
belts constituted a sort of sacred war bundle, and were
treated as such. The drum keeper had charge of these items
when they were not in use.

The drum and its four supporting stakes were also regarded
as sacred and were carefully kept out of reach of children and
inebriates. In the Big Grass Dance the drum was of native
construction, usually made of an old style wooden washtub with
cowhide heads tacked on top and bottom and a colorful cloth
decoration tacked about the sides. It was provided with four
harness leather loops, spaced about the sides. These loops
could be hooked over projections on the four support stakes so
as to hold the drum about four inches above the ground when
the stakes were driven into the earth. The support stakes
bowed out gracefully at the top and were wrapped with beadwork, ribbons, or red cloth. They were often decorated with
eagle feathers or bull tails hanging from the tips, which
vibrated when the drum was struck.

To initiate a performance of the Big Grass Dance the drum
keeper carried or sent small pouches of tobacco to each of the
officers. Their acceptance was a pledge that they would
appear on the appointed day. The announcer also went about

notifying members of the group and the camp at large of the coming event and its purpose. Most often the dance was staged for the benefit of some destitute person or family, although the regular spring and fall dances might be staged regardless of any such objective. If any of the officers of the society failed to appear, they were fined by the society.

The drum keeper, drum warmer, and four male singers were generally the first to arrive at the dance hall. The drum was warmed to tighten the heads, hung in place at the center of the hall, and the singers began. At first the drum was tapped softly and the songs sung in a low voice. At this time the singers might refresh their memories concerning the ritually prescribed songs or might learn new songs of the ordinary type. The women singers, as they arrived, ranged themselves in an arc behind the men. They sang an octave above the men. On certain songs the head singer raised his drum stick in the air. This was a signal for the men to remain quiet on the second part of the song and let the soaring voices of the women finish it. There was much good natured joking if the women missed their cue on unfamiliar songs.

As the other participants and spectators arrived, the singing became louder. Finally some young dancer, bolder than his fellows, stood and danced out into the circle. He was soon followed by others, and the clashing of their heavy ankle bells blended with the beat of the drum, spurring the singers to greater efforts. More dancers arrived and joined in and soon the hall was filled with weaving and gliding dancers, their heavily beaded costumes catching the light, the long porcupine hair on their roach headdresses shaking, and the fringes on their shirts and trousers swaying to accentuate their movements.

During the first part of the ceremony most of the dances were open to all male participants. The exceptions were certain giveaway songs requested by one or another family for some special purpose. For example, if a man had been newly appointed as an officer of the Big Grass Dance society, he and his family danced alone, assisted by their relatives and friends. After this dance they presented through the announcer gifts of cash, blankets, quilts, and yard goods to the singers, other officers of the society, friends, or honored guests from other tribes. These dances, known as "specials," were announced in advance by the society's announcer, a man selected for his fine speaking voice, knowledge of the protocol of the dance, acquaintance with most of the people present, and often for his ability to make witty remarks that put people in a pleasant, festive mood.

If, during the dancing, one of the dancers dropped an eagle feather or bell or other item of costuming, the general dancing stopped as soon as the accident was noticed. The singers struck up a special song used only for this purpose and a single dancer selected for this duty, usually an experienced warrior, danced around the fallen object and picked it up. In the days of intertribal warfare he sometimes pretended to stalk the fallen item as if it were an enemy, striking it with his dance stick as if to count coup. In the more recent past he merely retrieved it and returned it to its owner. He might then recite some important incident in his life, such as an experience in war. The person who dropped the item was expected to make a donation to the singers or to someone else in the assembled group in payment for the retrieved item.

Important in maintaining the vigor and enthusiasm of the dancers were the two whip men, who were seated on either side of the entrance. As each song began they rose and danced before the seated dancers, one moving clockwise and the other counterclockwise. Each carried a special type of notched club whip with an otter fur or fox skin wrist guard. As they passed around the circle, the seated dancers were expected to rise and join the dance. When the two whip carriers met at the back of the hall they turned and danced side by side toward the drum. If any dancer was still seated after the two whip carriers met, the whip carrier in charge of that side of the hall danced back to see what was wrong. Formerly, it is said, laggard dancers were actually whipped across the legs but in more recent years the function of the whip carriers was only symbolic.

During the dancing the drum keeper, when not dancing himself, remained seated at the place of honor at the back of the hall. The five crow belts were hung on the wall behind him. On the bench beside him was a tobacco box and a large catlinite pipe. At any time during the dance when the singers wished to rest and smoke, the drum keeper filled the pipe and carried it to them. After this anyone was allowed to smoke. A bucket of water and a dipper might be carried to the singers and dancers at this time as well.

When the general dancing had continued past the middle of the afternoon, the concluding parts of the Big Grass Dance ceremony were performed. Up to this time no eating was allowed, and if anyone should bring in some food and eat it, he might be taken to the center of the hall and made to consume a huge bucket of greasy soup, or to eat a large raw onion. The same penalty was exacted of an officer who arrived late. Small children, however, were excluded from this rule. Just before the concluding part of the ceremony, ten songs were sung during which everyone was expected to dance. Usually all danced enthusiastically during these ten songs, as they knew they would have a long rest afterward while the officers performed their ritual acts.

The concluding parts of the dance then followed. First the singers intoned the "take down the crow belts" song. This was danced by the two waiters or servers who were seated on either side of the entrance just inside the whip carriers. The song was sung four times. On each rendition the two servers rose and danced completely around the hall. On each round, as they passed the row of crow belts hanging on the wall at the back of the hall, they raised their arms, palms outward, toward the belts--a sign of great respect. At the end of the fourth rendition of the song the two servers took down the five belts one at a time, fumigated them over a pan of live coals on which sweetgrass had been placed, and laid them out on blankets spread on the ground. The two servers then knelt and tied on their own belts by means of the attached woolen sashes. The other three purified belts were given to the big forked spit carrier, the spoon carrier, and the "wounded warrior." This last official was given the belt with the red-dyed feathers. These officers did not tie on their bustles, yet, however, but remained seated holding the ornaments in front of them.

Next, one of the waiters took a pail containing cooked dog meat, which had been prepared ahead of time, and placed it near the center of the dance hall, just west of the drum. The other took the "enemy warrior" with his red-painted wooden gun and seated him near this pail. The waiters then took their seats.

The big forked spit carrier, the spoon carrier, and the wounded warrior went to the blankets spread on the ground and placed their crow belts on them, each kneeling behind his ornament and facing east. Then the singers intoned the "tightening of the crow belts" song. Like other songs in the concluding part of the Big Grass Dance, it was sung four times. On the first rendition the three officers merely sat erect. On the second they rose on their knees and swayed from side to side. When the crow belts were mentioned in the song, they extended their arms forward in an attitude of respect, as noted before. On the third rendition they picked up their belts and rose. Holding the bustles before them, they danced clockwise around the hall. As they passed the entrance, the two waiters rose and followed, all dancing single file to the back of the hall where the three remaining officers tied on their crow belts. On the fourth rendition all five danced around the pail of soup. At this point the "enemy" maneuvered behind the pail, pointing his wooden gun at the "wounded warrior" bringing up the rear. This man dodged but finally fell as if hit. Someone in the crowd who had actually rescued a comrade under fire came and picked up the fallen man. After the "wounded warrior" had been assisted to his feet and led away, the other four crow belt wearers filed past the pail, each tapping the rim as an act of counting coup. This episode ended with the "wounded warrior" and his rescuer coming to the center of the hall to relate how and where they had performed the actual deeds that they had re-enacted.

The next formal song was danced by the spoon carrier. He went back and forth toward the pail of dog soup three times. On the fourth rendition he picked it up and offered it symbolically to the four Thunderbirds or four world quarters. Having done this he carefully set it down again.

Prior to the fourth song the five officers wearing the crow belts were positioned around the pail of dog soup. Three knelt on one side, two on the other. Each untied his crow belt and placed it before him. During the four renditions of the song they sat erect, knelt, stood, and finally danced around the kettle holding their belts before them.

On the fifth song the big forked spit carrier rose and tied on his crow belt once again; then the other four followed. He

led them around the hall four times, each time returning to
the pail of dog soup. As they passed by the pail, each man
held his right arm extended over it, palm outward. At the end
of the song all five resumed their original seats at the sides
of the hall. The big forked spit carrier and the spoon carrier were seated on either side of the drum keeper at the rear
of the hall, and the "wounded warrior" was also seated in this
area. The two waiters, as noted earlier, were seated just inside the whip carriers near the entrance.

Next came the most dramatic and exciting episode of the Big
Grass Dance, the c'eht'ákpe 'charging the kettle'. It was
danced by the big forked spit carrier alone. The man selected
for this position must be a highly respected member of the
community and also an expert dancer. He took his name from
his implement of office, a spit or spear sharpened at one end,
with a fork at the other. Except for the sharpened point,
these objects were often completely covered with beadwork or
wrapped quillwork and had an eagle feather hanging from one of
the branches of the forked end. Smaller versions of this object were sometimes carried by the two waiters or servers.
To begin the dance, one of the servers went to the rear of
the hall and removed the big forked spit from its shelf. He
placed it in the right hand of the big forked spit carrier and
led him to his beginning station by holding the sharpened end.
The dance began near the entrance in front of the servers'
seats.

The singers then intoned the "spearing the dog's head"
song. The big forked spit man sat quietly through the first
rendition. On the second he rose and danced in place. Because this was the principal feature of the dance and a solo
part, all eyes were upon him. The crowd was tense and abso-
lute quiet prevailed.

As the song went into its third repeat the tempo increased and the dancer put more energy into his movements. He danced clockwise around the hall in front of the seated observers, using fancy steps and balancing the big forked spit in his right hand, well away from his body. By the fourth repeat the dancer had worked himself into a frenzy. Dancing back and forth toward the pail, he gestured with his spear as if he were facing a real enemy. Finally, as the song neared its end, he plunged the point of the spit into the center of the pail, leaving it there. He danced a few circles around the kettle to finish the song and then resumed his seat.

The head singer and drum keeper went to the pail to examine its contents. The traditional dog soup of the Grass Dance was prepared using the flesh of a puppy that had not been allowed to become a family pet. The dog was ritually strangled with a rope by two men, then singed over an open fire to remove the hair. It was butchered, washed in several waters, and the flesh cut into pieces about three inches square. These pieces of meat, together with the dog's skull, were placed in a pail of water and boiled without salt. In his dramatic dance the big forked spit carrier attempted to spear the dog's skull. If the spit pierced the skull, every officer was expected to give something away. If he failed to pierce the head but speared another piece of meat, it was presented to the head singer, who bit it off the end of the spit while it was held over his head.

Following the excitement of the big forked spit carrier's dance, there was a special pipe song. The drum keeper carried the pipe to the singers and everyone smoked and relaxed for a short while. Water was carried to both singers and dancers by the two servers.

Next came the "spoon song." Four respected old warriors were selected from the group and were seated by the two

servers near the pail of dog soup. Each held a wooden feast
bowl. The singers took up the "spoon song" and the spoon carrier rose and danced. He made four rounds of the hall, one
for each rendition of the song. At the end of the last one he
stopped before the four old warriors. Using his implement of
office, a quilled or beaded wand with a small spoon carved at
one end, he dipped into the kettle and brought out a tiny portion of the soup for each of the four men, touching the lips
of each in turn with the spoon. This was considered a high
honor. After this, more substantial portions of the dog soup
were poured out for each of the four men. The dog's head was
placed in one of the four feast bowls. Other food was also
brought out and placed on the ground near the drum. On the
next song all present stood up and danced in place holding
their feast bowls or other dishes in their hands. Then everyone ate, the singers and dancers being served first.

While the individuals who were served last finished their
meal, the waiters removed the dog's skull from the dish of the
older warrior to whom it had been given and placed it on the
floor between the drum keeper's seat at the back of the hall
and the drum and singers in the center. The remainder of the
dog soup in the pail was poured into four feast bowls placed
in a row between the skull and the drum. Then four warriors,
different men from the four who had been fed by the spoon
carrier, were brought forward and seated, one behind each
bowl.

The singers began the "dog's head eating song." During
this song each of the four warriors danced in turn around the
skull, which represented an enemy, and re-enacted one of his
valorous deeds. When each had finished he returned to his
place and ate his bowl of dog soup. Only one song was used
for all four performances. Generally each person who danced

donated food or money for the next Big Grass Dance performance. At this stage of the dance it was also customary for
anyone who wished to do so to stand and announce contributions
for the next dance, whether he had danced or not. These donations were made through the announcer, and there was generous applause when someone donated a hog or a beef or a large
sum of money.

When all who wished to give away something were finished,
the singers began the "going out the door song," the last song
of the ceremony. It was sung the customary four times and no
one was allowed to enter or leave the hall while it was being
sung. On the fourth rendition the "wounded warrior" moved to
the center of the floor. He untied his crow belt and maneuvered it about, pointing it toward the closed door, now symbolizing the enemy lines. As the song ended he rushed for the
door and opened it, making a path for the rest of the crowd.
So the dance ended.

The above account is an idealized and somewhat generalized
description of a Big Grass Dance performance in its heyday.
In this form the dance was transmitted by the Canadian and
U.S. Sioux to the Plains Ojibwas, Plains Crees, and Assiniboines, and this description applies equally well to their
performances. The Plains Ojibwas and Plains Crees term it
the "Sioux Dance" to indicate the tribe of origin. Although
there are still a few singers who can sing the full roster of
songs from the Big Grass Dance in proper order (Eli Taylor,
Sioux Valley; Robert Good Voice, Round Plain; John Goodwill,
Standing Buffalo), this formal version of the dance has been
obsolete among the Canadian Sioux for many years, probably
since the 1930s. It is still staged by the Plains Ojibwas at
Swan Lake, Manitoba, twice a year, another example of a borrowing tribe continuing a Sioux ceremony after it has been

abandoned by the lenders. The last Sioux performance of the
full Big Grass Dance ritual was staged in 1969 by singers and
dancers from Standing Buffalo Reserve at the request of Sam
Corrigan, an anthropologist from Brandon University.

As would be expected in such a lengthy and complicated
ceremony, there were many variations in the ritual as performed from one Canadian Sioux reserve to the next. Thus Arthur
Young (Oak Lake) gave the sequence of ritual acts in the latter part of the dance as follows:

> 1st song: Big forked spit carrier searches in
> the cupboard of the dance hall for the pot contain-
> ing the dog soup and dog's head. When he finds it
> he carries it to the center of the floor of the
> dance hall.
> 2nd song: He dances around the pot.
> 3rd song: He spears the dog's head with his
> forked spit.
> 4th song: The spoon carrier feeds dog soup to
> certain warriors.

Robert Good Voice (Round Plain) gave the following:

> 1st song: Crow belts are taken down and pre-
> pared.
> 2nd song: Crow belt wearers pick up and put on
> the crow belts.
> 3rd song: The pail containing dog soup is
> brought to the middle of the dance floor. The
> four dancers dance toward it as if they were ap-
> proaching an enemy. At the end each touches the
> pail.
> 4th song: The spoon carrier dips his spoon into
> the soup and offers a piece of meat to the cardinal

points, east, south, west, and north. The food
is then passed out.

5th song: Everyone dances in place holding his
plate or bowl of food.

6th song: Crow belt wearers dance and then donate to the poor. Later others can do this as well.

Mr. Good Voice recorded some of the ritual songs. The
words to the song used for preparing the crow belts (1st
song) are:

K'odá waŋ yuhápi t'ehíke

Friend, it is difficult wearing this [crow belt].

The song used when the crow belt wearers pick up and put on
the belts (2nd song) is:

K'aŋgíha waŋ škáte do.
Heyúska waŋ škáte do.

The crow belt is now in play.
Members of the Heyuska, it is now in play.

The song used when the crow belt wearers charge the kettle
(3rd song) has these words:

Dé yuhána natáŋpi.
Dé yuhána natáŋpi, k'odá.
P'ejíŋ hoksína kiŋ, k'odá.

They are charging with them.
They are charging with them, friend.
It is the Grass [Dance] boys, friend.

The song used when everyone dances in place with his bowl
of food (5th song) has this simple text:

Heyúska wótape.

Members of the Heyuska, eat!

According to Mr. Good Voice there were only four men who
wore the crow belt ornament, not five.

The most complete description I recorded among the Canadian
Sioux of the Big Grass Dance was provided by John Goodwill
(Standing Buffalo), who included the ancillary Warbonnet Dance
in his account:

> In the old form of the Grass Dance the drum
> keeper was always a young man. There were four
> drummers [singers] only. Only men danced. Four
> men wore the crow belt. The members of the soci-
> ety were invited by the crier when a dance was go-
> ing to be held. Once they assembled in the hall
> there was an announcer for the men's side and
> another for the women's side.
>
> 1. They generally began with a few ordinary
> Grass Dance songs to warm up.
>
> 2. Next they hung up four warbonnets behind a
> man called the wap'áha yuhá ['warbonnet keeper'].
> These warbonnets were taken down and put on by
> four women who danced the Warbonnet Dance. These
> women were called Tac'ó it'ąc'aŋ ['Tac'ó leaders'].
> The warbonnets were then put on four other women
> who led the dance, and so on. After each set of
> four women had worn the warbonnets in the dance,
> they would donate. This was to raise money for
> whatever purpose had been announced. The words
> of one of these songs are:
>
> Tac'ó it'ąc'aŋ itúh'aŋpi c'a isí waníce.
> Nit'á óksaŋ oháŋk'esni óta ye.
>
> The Tac'ó leaders are donating but they do not
>   expect any return gifts.
> Many of you around here are needy.

After this series of songs the announcer thanks
the people for their donations.

3. More general Grass Dance songs follow.

4. A few rounds of the Kahómni may be danced
at this time.

5. A T'at'áŋka Wac'ípi ['Buffalo Bull Dance']
may be danced.

6. A small kettle containing the heart or
tongue of a beef or a young dog is placed in the
center of the floor at the east end of the dance
hall in preparation for the c'eht'ákpeyapi ['charging of the kettle']. After this there is a
c'ehyáwapi ['counting of kettles']. Each person
has brought a contribution to the feast, consisting of five bannocks, a pot of tea, a pail of
Saskatoon berries, or the like. These are arranged
in the central area by the Omáha it'áŋc'aŋ ['Omaha
leaders', the leaders on the men's side] and the
Tac'ó it'áŋc'aŋ ['Tac'ó leaders', the leaders on the
women's side]. As each person comes forward he
announces what he has brought. He pays a fine if
he has come empty handed.

Next, the pot containing the dog or beef is
smudged with sweetgrass. Now the singers begin
the "charging the kettle songs." A man called the
wiyóknak wic'ák'ita or "feeder" [the big forked
spit carrier] begins to dance. First he merely
stands in place. Next he dances around the kettle.
On the third song his dancing becomes livelier.
On the fast part of the tail of the third song he
swoops down over the kettle and spears a piece of
meat with his fork. On the fourth song he serves
it to the drum keeper.

When this is all finished they sing the crow belt songs.

7. Kneeling, the four crow belt wearers raise their hands over the belts, which are spread over benches.

8. On the next song they put the belts on.

9. On the third song of this series they dance wearing the belts.

10. The fourth song is the serving song. Its words are:

Wanâ wakápta dowáŋ po.

Now sing the serving song!

On this song two of the four Omâha it'áŋc'aŋ dance around the food, which is in the center. As they pass it they hold their right hands extended over it as an act of blessing. There are four verses. At the end they go to the announcer and announce donations. Then they serve the assembled food. When it has all been distributed they say, Wanâ wóta po 'Now eat!' Each dance club has a police-man who has a large pipe. If anyone eats before the Omâha it'áŋc'aŋ tell the people to begin, the offender must smoke a big pipeful of strong plug tobacco and kinnikinnick. Their relatives might "pay them off" by donating to the society, however.

At the end of the dance there was a feature called k'ináp'a odówaŋ 'going out song'. One man dances in a circle four times. At the end of the fourth song he opens the door and the people go out.

The above description of the Big Grass Dance is particularly interesting in that it places the preparation and donning
of the crow belts after the charging of the kettle feature, an
unusual variation.

The final account of the formal Grass Dance was secured
from Pete Lethbridge (Wood Mountain), and describes the Teton
version seen there:

> At Wood Mountain we call the Grass Dance <u>Omáha</u>
> <u>Wac'ípi</u>. The last Omaha Dance we had at Wood Moun-
> tain was about forty years ago [1932]. We are too
> few now. Jim Le Caine used to have an adobe dance
> hall at his place and we used to hold our dances
> there. Dances I remember are the <u>Omáha</u> with the
> <u>c'eht'ákpe</u> ['charging of the kettle']. After the
> man with the spear [big forked spit carrier] had
> charged the kettle, he dipped a feather in the
> soup and offered it to the four directions. Then
> he presented the end of the wet feather to a war-
> rior, a man whom he called "uncle." This man
> licked the soup from the end of the feather. Be-
> fore the charging of the kettle there were songs
> for taking down and fumigating the crow belts.
> The crow belts are so called because every feather
> stands for a dead Crow Indian. They hate to see
> these.

The interpretation of the name and symbolism of the crow belt
as given by Mr. Lethbridge is, of course, idiosyncratic. The
ornament was originally named for the stuffed crow skin that
was present in the older form, the crow being one of the
guardians of Sioux warriors.

It is interesting to note that although it is contrary to all historical evidence, today some Sioux and Assiniboines believe that the Grass Dance originated in the north. Thus Frank Merrick (Long Plain) stated that the dance had been originated by a young Sioux who dreamed of a rooster dancing. He copied the costume for the dance from the comb and tail feathers of the rooster in his vision. Ernest White Eagle (age 92, Fort Belknap, Montana), an Assiniboine, claimed a joint Sioux and Assiniboine origin for the dance:

> The P'ejíŋ Wac'ípi ['Grass Dance'] is also called P'ejíŋ Miknáka ['Grass Tucked-in']. The name refers to bunches of grass originally worn in the belts of the dancers. The word Heyúska also occurs in certain songs and seems to be another name for the dance. I think it is an Assiniboine word but I do not know its meaning. This dance was originated many years ago jointly by my tribe and the Dakota at a place between Gull Lake and Shaunavon, Saskatchewan. At this time they made a drum with its top painted blue and yellow. The yellow symbolized the sun. The drum had material tacked to the side, also a white fur strip near the top. It was supported on four curved stakes with beadwork, horsetails, and eagle feathers. The stakes had hooks to hold the drum. At this meeting the dance was explained to all present, the various officers assigned, and all present were told to take the dance home. At that time it was predicted by an old man that the dance would spread to all tribes. Now this prediction seems to be coming true.

Some old customs of the Grass Dance, not noted above, are the "whistle custom," "dancing the tail," and "release from mourning." The whistle custom involves certain dancers (generally there were only two in any Grass Dance society) who carry a long wooden whistle carved at the end to represent the head of a screaming crane. These whistles are called siyót'aŋka 'big prairie chicken'. When the singers are rendering a particularly good song, these whistle carriers have the privilege of leaning over the musicians and blowing their whistles over their heads on the last chorus. When this occurs, the singers must repeat the song, and must continue to repeat it as often as the whistle carrier sounds his signal at the appropriate point. This is generally done four times, the sacred number, but to do this more than four times is considered bad form. The whistle custom is still a part of the Grass Dance today, and I observed it at several powwows in Manitoba and Saskatchewan during the summer of 1972.

"Dancing the tail" refers to the practice by which two men, specially selected for their skill as dancers, dance alone during the "tail" of the song. Grass Dance songs are in two parts, an initial phrase and a shorter second part, termed the tail. After several renditions of both parts of a song, the singers will stop for a few seconds, then sing the tail part again. It is on this final rendition of the tail that the tail dancers rise from their seats again and dance. Originally only warriors who had gone out under fire in battle and rescued a fallen comrade would be selected as tail dancers. This custom is now obsolete.

The release from mourning custom involves the restoration or reincorporation into society of a mourner at a Grass Dance performance. This person, still dressed in shabby clothing and with uncombed hair, is seated on a blanket spread on the

floor near the drum. At a certain point in the dance the
mourner is given new, bright clothing, his face is washed and
painted and his hair is combed. Two dancers then raise the
bereaved person up and he is told to enjoy life once more.
This custom is still observed.

Formerly, according to Robert Good Voice (Round Plain),
there was an initiation by ordeal for those men wishing to
join the Grass Dance society. This involved setting fire to
the bunches of dry grass worn in the belts of the dancers.
The candidate must dance one song with this grass burning. A
man's sisters and female parallel cousins (also called sisters
in the Sioux kinship system) could, however, use their hands
to put out the fire for their brother. Mr. Good Voice also
mentioned that formerly officials were expected to donate
heavily to pay for their positions in the society. A man selected as one of the whip carriers, for example, must have
stolen four horses from the enemy and have given at least
three of these to the poor.

At the present time, since they are fully clothed, Grass
dancers only paint their faces, if they wear any paint at all.
In the latter part of the nineteenth century, however, dancers
often were naked except for breechcloth and ornaments. In
those days, according to Charles Padani (Standing Buffalo),
the dancers often rubbed their hands with red or black paint
and then applied colored hand prints to their bodies. Another
old type of body paint was to color the face and lower arms
black.

Today the Grass Dance has shed most of its ritual features,
and women and children join in it with the men. It is performed mainly to provide entertainment for the dancers, singers, and spectators. It also allows modern Sioux, as well as
other tribesmen, to express their pride in being Indian and to

meet one another in an Indian atmosphere. But even today, the songs are still in the characteristic Grass Dance style, and the traditional man's roach headdress and crow belt are very much in evidence.

The Sioux are acknowledged to be the liveliest Grass Dancers in Canada, and every reserve community, if it can possibly find the resources to do so, sponsors an inter-tribal powwow each summer, inviting dancers and singers from far and near to come and dance and feast with them. Cash prizes, awarded for the best dancing and costuming in various classes determined by age and sex, draw participants from distant points in Canada and the United States.

Typically, such a powwow is held under a "big top" or circus tent rented for the purpose. Various singing groups, both local and visiting, position themselves around the margins of the tent. These singing groups change off with one another, in rotation, to provide the music for the clockwise circuit of the dancers, who often number in the hundreds. Each dancer, beautifully arrayed in his or her most gorgeous costume, is free to choose individual steps and style of dancing. At the same time, each maintains the rhythm of the singing and the drum. When the final drumbeat of a particular song sounds, it coincides exactly with the final clash of the dancers' bells.

Grass Dance music is martial and exciting, reflecting the warrior society origins of the dance. Rhythm of drum and voice, although geared to one another, are nevertheless somewhat independent, providing a syncopated effect. Formerly, in the Big Grass Dance, many songs had words telling of warlike deeds or generosity of members of the society. Today, most songs employ only vocables or burden syllables. Each song is repeated several times, then ended. After a short pause, the second part of the song, the tail, is presented. Formerly, at this point, the song was concluded. Today, however, it is the custom to start the song over again and sing it through several times more. This is a modern powwow phenomenon, frowned upon by purists. It results from the presence of several "drums" or singing groups, each singing in rotation. Knowing that once they have finished they will not be called upon to sing again for perhaps two hours, they prolong their song as long as possible in order to "hold the drum." Often one song may be continued for as long as a half hour, whereas formerly five minutes was the average length for a single song. The whistle custom also acts to lengthen songs.

New songs are composed and introduced each season, and better songs soon became a part of the standard repertoire. Visiting singers and dancers often make tape recordings of these new songs and bring them back to their home communities. Thus a song composed on a reserve in Manitoba or Saskatchewan begins its diffusion, and in the course of a year or two may turn up at powwows in such far flung locales as Oklahoma, Arizona, or Washington. Costume and dancing styles also spread at these intertribal powwows. Thus the so-called Oklahoma fancy dance style of costume and dancing, featuring staccato footwork and elaborate stylized shoulder and back bustles of feathers, reached Manitoba in 1970, and seems to threaten to displace the older Northern style of costume and dancing (cf. Howard 1955b, 1960f). At the powwows I attended in the summer of 1972 (Prince Albert, Beardy's Reserve, Fort Qu'Appelle, and White Cap in Saskatchewan; Sioux Valley and Fort Garry in Manitoba), skillful exponents of both Northern and Oklahoma fancy dance styles could be seen. Whatever its musical or choreographic transformations, it is apparent that the Grass Dance, in its contemporary powwow setting, is a vigorous and vital art form, a characteristic cultural expression of native North America.

Tac'ó, Warbonnet, and Buffalo Dances

There are other dances of a ceremonial nature that were formerly performed together with the Grass Dance. The first of
these, the Tac'ó Wac'ípi, seems to be a reservation era development out of the old Iwákic'i Wac'ípi ('Praise Dance'),
the Victory or Scalp Dance. Wallis (1947:42-49) describes
this dance society as he observed it in 1914 at Sioux Village,
although he seems to have confused it with the Big Grass
Dance. (Compare the Assiniboine account in Long [1961:121-
23].) The society was essentially a women's group, although
certain men also belonged to it. Four of the women danced
with whistles and staffs, according to Charles Padani (Standing Buffalo). The choreography was that of the old Victory
Dance, namely a quick step to the left, dancers facing the
center.

The Wíyaka Wap'áha Yuhpá Wac'ípi or Warbonnet Dance was
also performed in connection with the Grass Dance, as described by John Goodwill, above. I saw this dance in 1951
performed by Yanktonais on Standing Rock Reservation in North
Dakota. A file of male dancers, the leader wearing a warbonnet, moved clockwise around the drum, with a file of female
dancers, their leader also warbonneted, inside going the opposite direction. The step for both sexes was a simple toe-heel
left, toe-heel right forward progression. While this was going on a single dancer, an "enemy scout," danced around the
outside of the two files of dancers, moving in a furtive manner. Soon a second single dancer appeared, a "Sioux warrior."
Toward the end of the song he engaged in mock combat with the
"enemy scout" and pretended to shoot him. The "enemy" fell as
if dead and was carried off by two other "warriors" and the
dance ended with the male and female warbonnet wearers an-
nouncing donations. The Canadian Sioux version of the dance

was probably much the same, except that two men and two women, the first and second in each file, wore warbonnets and donated.

The T'at'áŋka Wac'ípi 'Buffalo Bull Dance' was also performed in connection with the Grass Dance. Purely social in nature in later years, the dance seems originally to have been of a religious or warrior society type (cf. Wallis 1947:58-64). The dance imitates the movements of a herd of bison and their characteristic stamping gait. The songs of this dance, and its choreography, are virtually identical with those of the Southern Plains Buffalo Dance. The dancers are called to the floor by a tremolo of the drum. The singers then begin the song proper and the rhythm changes to a slow accented beat, upon which the dancers, facing the center of the floor, tread in place. On musical cue they trot a few steps to the left and tread again in place, the tremolo beat being the signal to trot off again. A group of men and women performing this dance have an uncanny resemblance to a herd of bison grazing, bunching up, and then stopping to graze again. This impression would have been heightened by the former custom of the male dancers wearing headdresses of bison scalps with horns.

Heyoka Dance

Another feature of the Grass Dances until a few years ago was the appearance of a Heyók'a or Clown dancer (see Howard 1954b). These clowns were always individuals who had dreamed of the Thunderbird, and as a result of their vision felt compelled to dress in the ridiculous costume and mask of the Heyoka or anti-natural god, and to do foolish things. Wallis was so fascinated with the Heyoka during his 1914 study of the Canadian Santees that more than half of his published monograph is devoted to the Clown cult (1947:111-223). Only one of my informants was alleged to be a member of the order. John Goodwill (Standing Buffalo) described this man as follows:

We have one man here who is a Heyoka. He became such because of a dream. As I understand it [from the recital of the dream given during a curing session] he did not dream of the Thunder but of a magpie, or at any rate the word he used in referring to his dream guardian was similar to the word for magpie. As a result of his dream he acted backward. Once when he was ice fishing with some of his relatives his cousin asked him to cut a small hole in the ice. Since he was a Heyoka he cut a huge one instead and flooded the ice where they were fishing.

On another occasion his daughter was baking bread. She asked him to bring in a few sticks of wood and to put them down gently by the stove so that her bread wouldn't fall. Of course, since he was a Heyoka, she should have told him to bring a lot of wood and throw it down hard. Since she asked for a few sticks, and to put them down gently, he brought a huge load and dropped it heavily, causing her bread to fall.

This man can cure as a result of his dream. One winter I picked him up in town. My niece was a baby then and she was very sick. He offered to cure her, so I let him go ahead. He started to sing but then stopped and turned to a woman who was present and said, "You should have told me you were menstruating!" He could tell from his

mystic powers. She removed herself from the room
and he continued with his cure and cured my niece.
When he had finished he said, "You will not be sick
from now on." He was right. She has never been
sick a day since. She is a grown woman now and
has many children.

Later I visited with the man Mr. Goodwill had indicated to
be a Heyoka. He accurately described the costume and behavior
of a Clown but would not admit to being a member of the cult.
The Heyók'a Kága ['Heyoka Imitators'], he said, could make it
rain. Sam Buffalo (Round Plain) commented that the "charging
of the kettle" feature of the Grass Dance is sometimes called
Heyók'a wóskate 'playing Heyoka', because the clowns used to
dip their bare arms into the scalding water to recover the
beef heart or dog's head. A Yankton "charging of the kettle"
song that I recorded in South Dakota mentions the Heyoka in
its text. Kenneth Eastman (Oak Lake) remembered that a Heyoka wearing a ragged costume and a bladder mask used to appear
at Grass Dances on that reserve. He carried a crooked bow
and arrows and would dance between the beats of the song, not
in time with them. The Heyoka cult is presently moribund
among the Canadian Sioux, although the neighboring Plains O-
jibwas and Plains Crees still have large and active Clown
cults. In 1968 I observed a beautiful Plains Cree tipi
pitched at the powwow grounds at Standing Buffalo Reserve that
was decorated with pictographs of Clowns. The owner stated
that he was a Clown and that the tipi cover was painted to
correspond with his Clown vision.

Ghost Dance

The Ghost Dance, that famous revitalization movement of Prairie, Plains, Basin, and California groups, reached the Canadian

Sioux in Saskatchewan but not those in Manitoba. In Saskatchewan it was performed at Wood Mountain, White Cap, and Round
Plain, but not at Standing Buffalo. At Round Plain it still
persisted, in a modified form, as late as 1950, and there are
still a few individuals at that reserve who regard themselves
as adherents. Kehoe (1968) has written of the principal personalities and history of the Canadian Sioux Ghost Dance. Her
paper contains valuable historical data as well as the Saskatchewan Sioux origin legend for the religion (1968:298-299).
However, her data conflict with information I secured from
Saskatchewan Sioux informants on several points.

The Ghost Dance, in its classic form, was inspired by the
Paiute Indian prophet Wovoka, also known as Jack Wilson. Its
central feature was a four day dance, a version of the Round
Dance, in which the participants held hands and side-stepped
in a clockwise direction for several hours at a time. As the
dance continued the leaders or prophets would wave eagle wing
fans before the faces of the dancers, or shine mirrors in
their eyes. This, together with the hypnotic effect of the
singing and dancing, would sometimes induce a trance in a
dancer, who would be transported in his mind to the afterworld
where departed relatives would be seen living the old, happy
life of the prereservation era, and where bison and other game
were abundant (Mooney 1896). Following the Wounded Knee massacre in 1890, the dance lost much of its impetus among the
Teton Sioux in the United States, although in 1891 it was a-
dopted by the Yanktonais at Standing Rock Reservation (Francis
Zahn, Fort Yates, North Dakota, personal communication, 1957),
and in 1895 the Tetons of Wood Mountain Reserve were dancing
at the fork of Wood River, six miles northwest of the present
Gravelbourg, Saskatchewan (Laviolette 1944:119). It appears
to have been practiced by both Tetons and Yanktonais for some

years afterward, but gradually lost favor among both groups.
Pete Lethbridge indicated that it survived for some years
after the turn of the century at Wood Mountain, and Kehoe
(1968:302) cites Beatrice Medicine to the effect that it is
still performed, although infrequently, by a few Sioux in the
United States.

It was among the Santees of White Cap and Round Plain, however, that the dance persisted longest, although undergoing
successive alterations in form. Sam Buffalo (Round Plain)
provided me with the most complete account of the Ghost Dance
and its derivatives among the Saskatchewan Sioux. His father,
who is now deceased, was an active member of the group at
Round Plain. Mr. Buffalo stated:

> The Ghost Dance, in its original form, was ori-
> ginated in the States. Prominent Dakota involved
> in its spread were Šiyó Háŋska 'Tall Prairie Chick-
> en', T'at'áŋka Ptécana 'Short Bull', and Mat'ó
> Wanáhtaka 'Kicking Bear'. It came here in this
> form, with dancing in a circle. Later it changed
> to what we call Wac'ékiye Dowáŋpi 'Prayer Sing-
> ing'. This form involved singing but no dancing.
> Still later, about 1900, a Hóhe [Assiniboine] from
> Wolf Point, Montana, brought a modified version of
> the Ghost Dance to three localities up here that
> had already taken up the Wacekiya Dowanpi form.
> These three places were (1) the Isáŋt'i camp north
> of Prince Albert, where the airport is now; (2)
> T'íŋtamibena, Round Plain Reserve; (3) Wap'áhaska,
> White Cap Reserve.
>
> The Hóhe's name was Fred Robinson. He had re-
> ceived a vision in which he was told to modify the

Wacekiya Dowanpi. His version was called W6yaka
T'éca 'New Tidings'. It never came to Fort Qu'-
Appelle [Standing Buffalo]. Members wore a
wac'íŋhe, a twisted thong with an eagle feather at
the end; wasé ['vermillion paint'] from a small
packet; and used wac'áŋga ['sweetgrass']. All of
these were carried over from the earlier Wacekiya
Dowanpi and the still earlier Ghost Dance. The
songs were changed at this time. Some of the old
Wacekiya Dowanpi were later incorporated into the
Kahomni Dance.

Fred Robinson trained James White Cap and John
Birch in the Woyaka Teca religion. Both of these
men were from White Cap Reserve. Members here
[at Round Plain] were Ernest Good Voice, Red
Dancer, and Cook Iron Side.

A typical Woyaka Teca ceremony would go like
this: The group would meet at someone's house.
They would sit on the floor, in a circle. In the
middle of the floor was a small mound of earth.
Going from east to west across this circle was a
trail of red paint [wasé]. This symbolized the
c'aŋkú dúta or good red path. At the east end of
this path was a small wooden saucer containing a
coal. At the west end was a c'aŋdúpa [catlinite
pipe].

Each person had with him a W6yaka T'éca w6t'awe
['New Tidings medicine bundle']. When all were
assembled and in place, wac'áŋga [sweetgrass] was
ignited from the coal in the saucer and all of the
individual bundles were fumigated (w6t'awe
azíŋk'iya). Next the leader recited the origins

of the Ghost Dance. He would speak of atéyapi
['father'] Jack Wilson. Then they would sing three
songs and pass three buckets of food. After the
closing prayer a fourth bucket was passed. The
foods used were c'aŋpá sápa [blackberries], háza
[huckleberries], meat, corn, and rice cooked with
raisins.

Ghost Dance shirts were retained in both the
Wacekiya Dowanpi and the Woyaka Teca. I used to
have my father's shirt and one belonging to another relative. I gave these to Mary Marino at the
Department of Anthropology at [the University of
Saskatchewan in] Saskatoon for their museum. The
Ghost Dance shirt had changed from a "bullet
proof" to a "sin proof" garment (wówahtani iyók'ihe
sni) by the time it got here.

Red Dancer, one of the prominent members of the
Woyaka Teca, died in the afternoon. Shortly before his death he had a vision in which it was
told that part of the Woyaka Teca was false.

A part of Fred Robinson's vision said that all
people must be painted with wasé or they would not
be received in heaven. This was followed scru-
pulously by the Woyaka Teca members, and they even
exhumed some recently buried members to paint them.

Robert Good Voice, also of Round Plain Reserve, gave the
following account of the Ghost Dance and its derivatives:

The Ghost Dance came here. It was founded by
Jack Wilson. If you danced it you could see dead
relatives. Fred Robinson brought another version
to this reserve. It was called Woyaka Teca.

This man had had a vision in which he was told
that the Wacekiya Wohanpi was wrong. He painted
people with wasé. He was told to open graves and
put wasé on the bones. A local man who was prominent in the Ghost Dance was Joe Goodshield. Another was Waȟpézizi ['Yellow Leaf'].

Pete Lethbridge (Wood Mountain) commented as follows:

The Ghost Dance was performed at Wood Mountain.
The Wacekiya Wohanpi or Prayer Feast was derived
from it. I went to one of these once. Everyone
sat in a circle. Everyone called one another by
some kin term, such as brother or cousin. Then
each person prayed in turn. They prayed fast.
Then everyone was given a dish of grease bannock
and tea, and they had to eat this fast.

In all the versions above, it is apparent that the earlier
Medicine Dance and its ancillary rite, the Medicine Feast, had
a strong influence on the Wacekiya Wohanpi (Prayer Feast) and
the Woyaka Teca (New Tidings) Ghost Dance derivatives. In the
case of the Wood Mountain rite, this even included a variant
of the old Santee eat-all feast.

Sam Buffalo described Canadian Sioux Ghost Dance shirts as
being made of cloth with buckskin fringes. One he had seen
was yellow. All were decorated with Ghost Dance symbols, such
as the morning star, and each had an eagle claw attached to
the right shoulder.

I recorded four songs of the Prayer Feast, two from Robert
Good Voice (Round Plain) and two from Archie Eagle (White
Cap). They are all of the type used about 1908-1909. Mr.
Good Voice's songs have the following texts:

(1) Maȟpíya óksaŋ wahíyaye.
Maȟpíya óksaŋ wahíyaye.
Até t'ac'áŋdupa yuȟá wahíyaye.
Mak'óce óksaŋ wahíyaye.

I circle the heavens.
I circle the heavens.
Carrying my father's pipe I go.
I circle the country.

(2) Áŋpao wic'áŋȟpi até heyá hináp'e,
Wic'óicaǧe miyé wahínawap'e.

Father morning star said this as he appeared,
Giving life I appear

Mr. Eagle's songs have the following texts:

(1) Dé oyáte kiŋ mit'ác'aŋku kiŋ ognáye.
Dé até héye do.

This people follow my road.
The father said this.

(2) Até ektá c'éyaya mawáni.
Maȟpíya ektá hé t'aŋíŋyaŋ mawáni.
Mic'íŋkši katíŋyaŋ máni wo.

I walk crying to my father.
To heaven, openly I walk.
My son, walk straight!

Peyote Religion

The final religious system of Plains origins to be considered
in this chapter is the Peyote religion. Just as the Ghost
Dance did not reach the Sioux of Manitoba, so the Peyote religion has not as yet touched the Sioux in Saskatchewan,

although it has a large and enthusiastic following among the Plains Crees in that province. In Manitoba the Peyote religion was present on three of the four Sioux reserves (Sioux Village, Sioux Valley, and Oak Lake) in the late 1930s. It is no longer present anywhere except for a couple of members at Long Plain, the Plains Ojibwa reserve near Sioux Village where a few Sioux families are settled. These two individuals are of mixed Plains Ojibwa and Sioux descent.

It was apparently Tom Ross, a Yanktonai from Fort Totten, North Dakota, who introduced the Peyote way to the Canadian Sioux. According to Eli Taylor (Sioux Valley), who attended some of Ross's meetings, they were always "house meetings," that is, they were not held in the tipi commonly used for the peyote ceremony in the United States. This meant that the customary "V" shaped fire, usually a part of the central altar arrangement, was kept burning outside the house to provide the coals needed for burning the cedar incense, an important ritual act. Mr. Taylor thought it miraculous that a fire of two oak staves, burning only where they crossed, could burn all night through.

Although details are lacking, the ceremonial that Ross introduced among the Canadian Sioux was undoubtedly derived from Albert Hensley's Winnebago rite, a variant of the Big Moon or Cross Fireplace ritual (cf. La Barre 1938). Explanations of why the Peyote ritual failed to take hold among the Canadian Sioux are only conjectural, although the strength of other Christian churches and the distance from sources of peyote are probably relevant.

11. THE CANADIAN SIOUX TODAY

When one has visited Sioux communities in both the United
States and Canada, a comparison of the condition of the two
parts of the tribe, now citizens of separate nations, is in-
evitable. In such a comparison I would unhesitatingly state
that the Canadian Sioux, on the whole, seem to have fared the
better. Canadian Sioux homes tend to be better constructed
and maintained than their counterparts south of the border,
and their inhabitants, if not better off economically, certainly demonstrate a more positive attitude toward their government and the white world in general. The endless complaints about the Bureau of Indian Affairs and its treatment
of Indians, a constant theme in conversation with Sioux in the
United States, has no counterpart in Canada. There are exceptions, of course, but my evaluation tends to be shared by
both Canadian and U.S. Sioux who have had the opportunity to
visit both countries.

Reasons for the observed differential are harder to come
by. Certainly the factors cited by Kehoe (1970:151) are relevant: the lag in Canadian westward expansion as compared with
that of the United States, which gave Indian peoples more time
to adjust to the alien culture; and the mediating element of
the Métis. One is also inclined to credit the greater re-
sponsibility which, from the first, the Sioux refugees in
Canada were forced to assume for their own survival. During
the 1860s and 1870s, the Euro-Canadian settlers and their
government simply could not support large Indian populations
with rations. It was thus a question of individual initiative
for the Sioux refugees. Many died, but many others survived
through their own efforts.

The habits of frugality and hard work engendered in the
Sioux during these early years on Canadian soil, often as wage
laborers for non-Indian farmers and townsmen little better off
than themselves, seem to have served the Sioux well in subsequent years. Thus an inspector who visited Birdtail Reserve
in 1890 remarked: "I have not on any reserve seen so many
Indians so deligently [sic] employed (each one on his own
farm) at one time--the most remarkable point being, that as
they have no farmer to oversee them they set themselves to
work and pursue it with much judgement and industry" (quoted
in Meyer 1968:20). Although my interviews and observations
during the summer of 1972 were not specifically directed to
this question, the same "judgement and industry" evident
eighty-two years previously were still quite apparent on many
Canadian Sioux reserves.

The relatively small population aggregates, as compared to
the larger Sioux reservations in the United States, seem to
have worked for the good as well. Large surplus populations
in rural situations breed poverty on the larger Sioux reservations in the United States. Transportation costs militate
against bringing in anything but light industries to make use
of this potential labor force. In Canada, on the other hand,
the smaller reserve populations have made it possible for the
surrounding rural population to utilize, as farmhands and
laborers, any unemployed Sioux people not needed in farming
and cattle raising operations on the reserve. One might also
note that the tracts assigned for reserves in Canada are con-
siderably better for farming and grazing than reservation
lands in the United States.

In Canada, as in the United States, the smaller reserve
groups seem to have fared better than the larger ones. Thus
Chief William T. Eagle at White Cap Reserve (population 156)

noted that his people were quite well off, earning a liveli-
hood at farming and cattle raising, supplemented by some wage
labor for surrounding whites. He admitted that the appropri-
ation of a large part of the grazing land available to the
band by the nearby army camp had crippled the band's cattle
raising enterprise, but spoke enthusiastically of an attempt
to secure other land in its place. Chief Eagle was proud that
White Cap had been designated a model reserve a few years previously, and that the band had staged their yearly powwow on
their own, without benefit of government grant.

Francis Goodtrack, a young man of Wood Mountain Reserve
(population 70), was equally positive in his remarks about
that reserve's economic progress. Noting that conditions had
been poor in the 1940s and 1950s, he went on to remark:

> In 1962, for the first time, we elected a chief
> and council. Things have been better since then.
> New houses have been built and we have established
> a community pasture. We are proud of our housing
> program. Estimates are made of the cost of each
> unit required and money allocated by the federal
> government according to the amount needed and the
> amount available for the program. Indians are
> hired to assist in building the houses. Our re-
> serve is largely self-supporting. We have a mixed
> farming-cattle raising economic base here, and
> full employment.

When asked if alcoholism was a problem, Mr. Goodtrack said:

> Drinking is no problem here. Some young men
> drink, but only on payday, Saturday night. There
> is no racial discrimination here. Indian boys
> have white friends where they work. On Saturday

night they go out together and have a few drinks.
Sometimes the whole bunch, Indian and white, end
up sleeping off their celebration here on the reserve.

Conditions on the larger reserves such as Standing Buffalo
(population 512) and Sioux Valley (population 956) are not as
ideal, and unemployment is a problem, especially at the former. Since World War II the Canadian Sioux, like other small
farmers in the Plains, have suffered due to changes in the
patterns of agriculture. In the era of big farmers, the Indian, necessarily a small operator by virtue of the land
available to him, has been further handicapped by his inabili-
ty to use reserve lands as collateral for loans. The result
has been that the Sioux at Standing Buffalo have almost ceased
raising wheat and barley, formerly their principal cash crops.
All but four men on the reserve lease their lands and work at
wage labor. Their source of seasonal income as harvest hands
has also been reduced with the development of harvesting ma-
chines, hence many have been thrown onto relief rolls. Some
men are employed at the tuberculosis sanatorium in Fort Qu'-
Appelle, but many remain unemployed.

Joseph Goodwill (age 85), a patriarch of Standing Buffalo
Reserve, commented on this situation as follows:

I was a farmer here for forty years, until 1953.
The greatest change in my lifetime, for the Dakota
on this reserve, has been the move away from farming. Only four men farm now, but when I was a boy
everyone farmed or worked on a farm. A bunch of
Indian farmers would get together and hire a number of young men to help. We would work the farms
in rotation. This made for a friendly, cooperative

group and also served to interest the young men in farm work. We used ox-drawn plows. One man guided the oxen, another the plow. The plows were of wood. Planting was done by hand. Every family had a garden in those days as well. Today most don't. Fishing was also an important source of income. I used to go ice fishing two months each winter and sell the fish in town.

Farming remains the most important source of income at Sioux Valley, Birdtail, and Oak Lake reserves in Manitoba, supplemented by wage labor. Some Sioux have found jobs in the cities. Winnipeg, Brandon, Saskatoon, and Prince Albert all have Indian-Métis friendship centers where assistance in finding jobs, and sometimes a free or inexpensive meal, is provided for Indian job-seekers. Most unemployed Sioux, however, tend to stay on their reserves, recipients of provincial and federal welfare.

As in the United States, the Canadian government encouraged religious bodies to establish churches and mission schools on the reserves. There was a Presbyterian mission school at Birdtail as early as 1878. According to George Bear, the mission was served by a native Sioux minister, a Sisseton from South Dakota, who secured many Sioux converts. There was also a Church of England mission at Sioux Valley (then called Oak River) about the same time. Standing Buffalo Reserve acquired a Catholic day school in 1886. It lasted until 1895 when it was closed and the children went to a boarding school at nearby Lebret, founded in 1890 by the Oblate Fathers. This resulted in a large number of the Standing Buffalo band becoming Roman Catholics. A day school under Methodist auspices was operated at White Cap for about fifteen years, beginning in 1890 (Meyer 1968:22). These missions and mission schools

were and are powerful agents of White acculturation. Many
Sioux, of course, continued to practice their own religions.
The Medicine Dance persisted in Manitoba until at least 1930,
and the New Tidings derivative of the Ghost Dance continued to
be active at Round Plain until 1950. The Sioux, like many
American Indians, often simultaneously attend native religious
rites while maintaining membership in one or another Christian
church. Only the Evangelical church, which now has a strong
following at Standing Buffalo and Sioux Village, prohibits its
members from attending Indian dances and ceremonies.

On July 16, 1972, I attended the Sunday afternoon service
of an "All Nations Revival" sponsored by the Evangelical
church group at Standing Buffalo Reserve. This revival had
begun a few days earlier and was to conclude with the evening
service that day. The service was held in a large, much
patched circus-type tent that had been strung with electric
lights and equipped with folding chairs and benches. There
were about thirty Sioux present, a visiting Plains Ojibwa
couple, a white couple from Regina with their six musical
daughters, an older man (who identified himself as a former
Jewish rabbi) and his wife, and my wife and I.

Willie Isnana, a native minister, opened the services by
welcoming all present. A hymn followed, after which several
religious testimonials were presented, one by a visiting Oglala from Pine Ridge, South Dakota. The girls from Regina sang
next, accompanying themselves on guitars and accordians. One
guitar had the word "Hallelujah" painted on it in Gothic letters. Mr. Good Plume, a local Sioux, spoke next and introduced the young Oglala evangelist. This man delivered the
main sermon of the afternoon, emphasizing the power of faith
and God's redeeming love. He concluded by asking the congregation to join him in rendering "Amazing Grace." Other music

consisted of country and folk tunes such as "Red River Valley" with religious lyrics substituted for the original words. Frequently members of the congregation raised their right hands in response to telling points by the speaker. Twice during the afternoon service two teenage Sioux girls, wearing floor-length "granny" dresses, sang songs. They sang in the typical Sioux women's style, their mouths scarcely opened, their faces showing no emotion. The general tenor of the service was fervent and emotional. Following the service sandwiches and coffee were served in the adjoining house.

This Evangelical church, which apparently reached the Canadian Sioux by way of the Sioux at Fort Yates on Standing Rock Reservation, has gained numerous converts in the past few years. Sioux at both Round Plain and White Cap told me that relatives and friends were urging them to join. As noted earlier, the conversion of a large patrilineage at Sioux Village to this church has had the result of eliminating the summer powwow there. In addition to condemning Indian dances, the church is also violently opposed to the use of Indian herb medicines. However, church members are not opposed to producing beadwork or other Indian crafts for sale, and other Sioux scoff at this apparent inconsistency in their behavior.

A greater awareness of Indian identity has been evident among Canadian Sioux youth in recent years, according to my informants. I noted at the powwows I attended in 1972 that many young people wore headbands, long hair, and other badges of Indian militants in the United States, and displayed bumper stickers with such slogans as "Custer Died For Your Sins" and "This Is Indian Country." A concern with the loss of Sioux identity as expressed by the use of the Dakota language was evident at both Standing Buffalo and Round Plain, reserves at which there has been a great deal of intermarriage

with Plains Crees. Sam Buffalo, at Round Plain, initiated a
Dakota language course for young people in 1971, and planned
to continue it the following school year. Joseph Goodwill
(Standing Buffalo) commented:

> The young people here no longer speak Dakota in
> public. They may understand it, but they won't
> try to use it themselves. The boys are more re-
> luctant to speak Indian than the girls, somehow.
> The people at Sioux Valley are more Indian in this
> respect. I visited over there and was surprised
> to hear even little fellows talking Sioux.

In past years, in fact until after World War II, formal ed-
ucation for most Canadian Sioux was limited to grade school.
Since then more boys and girls are finishing high school and
some are going on to college, but drop-out rates are high. As
with the Sioux in the United States, it appears that there is
peer group pressure on the part of high school students against
any of their fellow Indian students excelling scholastically.
Because of this, one man at Sioux Valley said his daughter
prefers to attend school in Brandon, rather than locally, as
there are few fellow Indian students there to hold her back.

In summary, it might be said that Canada and the United
States, in their Indian policies, have pursued divergent roads
toward the same objective, namely, to bring their Indian populations to a point of economic and social equality with the
rest of the population. In regard to the Sioux people, neither country has succeeded. It is probably fair to say that
Canadian policy has had fewer obstacles to contend with, since
the settlement of the Canadian west was slower and the typical
settler was less land hungry and anti-Indian in sentiment.
Thus there are no Canadian parallels to the disastrous Dawes

Act (the General Allotment Act of 1887), which served to separate Indians in the United States from much of their land
base, or to the U.S. termination policies of the 1950s.

From 1970 until 1972 the Canadian Sioux attempted, as descendants of the Santees in the United States, to secure a
share in the Santee land claims settlement. My impression is
that most of the impetus behind this effort was the desire for
recognition as Santees by their U.S. cousins, not the hope of
securing large sums of money as such.

Only time will tell what the future holds for the Canadian
Sioux. Certainly there will be a slow but steady loss of
distinctively Sioux cultural features accompanied by a greater
identification as part of the larger entity of North American
Indians. At the present time, however, in spite of the loss
of a great deal of their traditional culture and its replace-
ment by features from the white man's world, their primary
identification is still as Sioux (Dakota or Lakota) and will
be so for many years hence.

APPENDIX: LIST OF INFORMANTS

Note: Age is indicated as of 1972. When exact age is not
known, the approximate age is an estimate by the author. Individuals whose names are marked with an asterisk (*) were
interviewed in 1958; estimated age is as of that date.

Name	Band Affiliation	Age	Reserve
George Bear	Yanktonai	93	Birdtail
Martin Bear	Yanktonai	65	Birdtail
Tom Brown	Wahpekute	60s	Oak Lake
Sam Buffalo	Wahpeton	40s	Round Plain
Archie Eagle	Sisseton	70s	White Cap
William T. Eagle	Sisseton	70s	White Cap
Kenneth Eastman	Wahpekute	83	Oak Lake
Robert Good Voice	Mdewakanton and Wahpeton	71	Round Plain
Kenneth Goodwill	Wahpeton and Teton	40s	Standing Buffalo
John Goodwill	Wahpeton and Teton	64	Standing Buffalo
Joseph Goodwill	Wahpeton	85	Standing Buffalo
Wayne Goodwill	Teton and Wah-peton	30s	Standing Buffalo
Simon Hanska	Mdewakanton	73	Birdtail
George High Eagle	Wahpekute	66	Oak Lake
Jim Kiyewakan	Sisseton/Wahpeton and Wahpekute	80s	Sioux Valley
Pete Lethbridge	Teton (Hunkpapa) and English	70s	Wood Mountain
Jim MacKay*	Sisseton	80s	Sioux Valley
Paul MacKay	Sisseton	72	Sioux Valley

Name	Band Affiliation	Age	Reserve
Frank Merrick	Sisseton (?) and White	87	Long Plain
Wallace Noel	Sisseton	40s	Sioux Valley
Hector Obie*	Sisseton	70s	Standing Buffalo
Charles Padani	Sisseton and Wahpeton	66	Standing Buffalo
Emma Pratt	Sisseton and Mdewakanton	88	Sioux Valley
Martha Tawiyaka	Sisseton	88	Standing Buffalo
Eli Taylor	Sisseton and Wahpeton	60s	Sioux Valley
Ernest White Eagle	Assiniboine tribe	92	Fort Belknap, MT
James Wounded Horse	Teton (Hunkpapa)	75	Wood Mountain
Arthur Young	Wahpekute	75	Oak Lake

BIBLIOGRAPHY

Corrigan, Samuel W.

    1970   The Plains Indian Powwow: Cultural Integration in
            Manitoba and Saskatchewan. Anthropologica, n.s.
            12:253-77.

Deloria, Ella

    1967   Some Notes on the Santee. Museum News of the W.H.
            Over Dakota Museum 28:1-21.

Deloria, Ella and Jay Brandon

    1961   The Origin of the Courting Flute: A Legend in the
            Santee Dakota Dialect. Museum News of the W.H. Over
            Museum 22:1-7.

Densmore, Frances

    1918   Teton Sioux Music. Smithsonian Institution, Bureau
            of American Ethnology, Bulletin 61.

Dole, Gertrude E.

    1972   Developmental Sequences of Kinship Patterns. In
            Kinship Studies in the Morgan Centennial Year.
            Priscilla Reining, ed. pp. 134-66. Washington,
            D.C.: Anthropological Society of Washington.

Eastman, Mary

    1849   Dahcotah; or, Life and Legends of the Sioux Around
            Fort Snelling. New York: John Wiley.

Fletcher, Alice and Francis LaFlesche

    1911   The Omaha Tribe. Smithsonian Institution, Bureau of
            American Ethnology, Annual Report 27.

Gilmore, Melvin R.

    1919   Uses of Plants by the Indians of the Missouri River
            Region. Smithsonian Institution, Bureau of American
            Ethnology, Annual Report 33, pp. 43-154.

Hodge, Frederick W., ed.

1907   Handbook of American Indians North of Mexico.
Smithsonian Institution, Bureau of American Ethnology, Bulletin 30, pt. 1.

Howard, James H.

1951   Notes on the Dakota Grass Dance. Southwestern Journal of Anthropology 7:82-85.

1954a   Yanktonai Dakota Eagle Trapping. Southwestern Journal of Anthropology 10:69-74.

1954b   The Dakota Heyoka Cult. The Scientific Monthly 78: 254-58.

1955a   The Tree Dweller Cults of the Dakota. Journal of American Folklore 68:169-74.

1955b   Pan-Indian Culture of Oklahoma. The Scientific Monthly 81:215-20.

1960a   The Cultural Position of the Dakota: A Reassessment. In Essays in the Science of Culture in Honor of Leslie A. White. Gertrude E. Dole and Robert L. Carneiro, eds. pp. 249-68. New York: Thomas Y. Crowell.

1960b   The Roach Headdress. American Indian Hobbyist 6:89-94.

1960c   Two Teton Dakota Winter Count Texts. North Dakota History 27:64-79.

1960d   Dakota Winter Counts as A Source of Plains History. Smithsonian Institution, Bureau of American Ethnology, Bulletin 173, Anthropological Paper 61, pp. 335-416.

1960e   When They Worship the Underwater Panther: A Prairie Potawatomi Bundle Ceremony. Southwestern Journal of Anthropology 16:217-24.

1960f   The Northern Style Grass Dance Costume. American Indian Hobbyist 7:18-27.

1961   The Identity and Demography of the Plains-Ojibwa.
        Plains Anthropologist 6:171-78.

1965   The Plains-Ojibwa: Hunters and Warriors of the
        Northern Prairies. University of South Dakota,
        Anthropological Papers of the South Dakota Museum 1.

1966a   The Dakota or Sioux Tribe: A Study in Human Ecology.
        University of South Dakota, Anthropological Papers
        of the Dakota Museum 2.

1966b   Dakota Interpretations of Bird Calls. Museum News
        of the Dakota Museum 27:19.

1968   The Warrior Who Killed Custer: The Personal Narra-
        tive of Chief Joseph White Bull. Lincoln: Universi-
        ty of Nebraska Press.

1972   Notes on the Ethnogeography of the Yankton Dakota.
        Plains Anthropologist 13:281-307.

1976   The Plains Gourd Dance As a Revitalization Movement.
        American Ethnologist 3:243-59.

1979   Some Further Thoughts on Eastern Dakota "Clans."
        Ethnohistory 26:133-40.

1980   The Dakota or Sioux Indians, A Study in Human Ecolo-
        gy. University of South Dakota, Anthropological
        Papers of the Dakota Museum 2. Reprint ed. with new
        preface, Lincoln: J & L Reprint.

Kehoe, Alice B.
1968   The Ghost Dance Religion in Saskatchewan, Canada.
        Plains Anthropologist 13:296-304.

1970   The Dakotas in Saskatchewan. In The Modern Sioux:
        Social Systems and Reservation Culture. Ethel
        Nurge, ed. pp. 148-72. Lincoln: University of
        Nebraska Press.

La Barre, Weston
1938   The Peyote Cult. Yale University Publications in
        Anthropology 19.

Landes, Ruth

1959   Dakota Warfare. Southwestern Journal of Anthropology 15:43-52.

1968   The Mystic Lake Sioux: Sociology of the Mdewakantonwan Santee. Madison: University of Wisconsin Press.

Laviolette, Gontran, O.M.I.

1944   The Sioux Indians in Canada. Regina: Marian Press.

Long, James Larpenteur

1961   The Assiniboines: From the Accounts of the Old Ones Told to First Boy (James Larpenteur Long). Michael Stephen Kennedy, ed. Norman: University of Oklahoma Press.

Lowie, Robert H.

1913   Dance Associations of the Eastern Dakota. American Museum of Natural History, Anthropological Papers 11:101-42.

Mayer, Frank B.

1932   With Pen and Pencil on the Frontier in 1851: The Diary and Sketches of Frank Blackwell Mayer. Bertha L. Heilbron, ed. St. Paul: Minnesota State Historical Society.

Meyer, Roy W.

1967   History of the Santee Sioux: United States Indian Policy on Trial. Lincoln: University of Nebraska Press.

1968   The Canadian Sioux: Refugees from Minnesota. Minnesota History 41:13-28.

Mooney, James

1896   The Ghost-Dance Religion and the Sioux Outbreak of 1890. Smithsonian Institution, Bureau of American Ethnology, Annual Report 14, pt. 2.

Neihardt, John G.

1961   Black Elk Speaks: Being the Life Story of a Holy
        Man of the Oglala Sioux. 1932. New ed., Lincoln:
        University of Nebraska Press.

Parker, John, ed.

1976   The Journals of Jonathan Carver and Related Docu-
        ments 1766-1770. St. Paul: Minnesota Historical
        Society Press.

Radisson, Peter Esprit

1943   Voyages of Peter Esprit Radisson. Gideon Scull, ed.
        New York: Peter Smith.

Riggs, Stephen R.

1893   Dakota Grammar, Texts, and Ethnography. James Owen
        Dorsey, ed. Contributions to North American Eth-
        nology 9. Washington, D.C.: Government Printing
        Office.

Skinner, Alanson P.

1919   A Sketch of Eastern Dakota Ethnology. American An-
        thropologist 21:164-74.

1920   Medicine Ceremony of the Menomini, Iowa and Wahpeton
        Dakota, With Notes on the Ceremony Among the Ponca,
        Bungi Ojibwa, and Potawatomi. Museum of the Ameri-
        can Indian, Heye Foundation, Indian Notes and Mono-
        graphs 4.

Thwaites, Reuben Gold, ed.

1959   The Jesuit Relations and Allied Documents, vol. 18.
        1896-1901. Reprint ed., New York: Pageant Books.

Tylor, Edward B.

1930   Anthropology: An Introduction to the Study of Man
        and Civilization, vol. 2. London: Watts.

Wallis, Wilson D.

1919   The Sun Dance of the Canadian Dakota. American
        Museum of Natural History, Anthropological Papers
        16:317-80.

1923   Beliefs and Tales of the Canadian Dakota. Journal
        of American Folk-Lore 36:36-101.

1947   The Canadian Dakota. American Museum of Natural
        History, Anthropological Papers 41, pt. 1.

Williamson, Thomas B.

1851   Dacotas of the Mississippi. In Information Respect-
        ing the History, Conditions, and Prospects of the
        Indian Tribes of the United States, vol. 1. Henry
        R. Schoolcraft, ed. pp. 247-56. Philadelphia.

Winchell, N.H.

1911   The Aborigines of Minnesota. St. Paul: Pioneer.

Woolworth, Alan R.

1969   A Disgraceful Proceeding: Intrigue in the Red River
        Country in 1864. The Beaver 299:54-60.

INDEX